T0129764

SLAVERY
to Nationhood

DR. JOHN THOMAS WYLIE

authorHOUSE®

AuthorHouse™
1663 Liberty Drive
Bloomington, IN 47403
www.authorhouse.com
Phone: 1 (800) 839-8640

Published by AuthorHouse 11/25/2019

ISBN: 978-1-7283-3769-2 (sc)
ISBN: 978-1-7283-3767-8 (e)

Print information available on the last page.

This book is printed on acid-free paper.

Scripture quotations marked KJV are from the Holy Bible, King James Version
(Authorized Version). First published in 1611. Quoted from the KJV Classic
Reference Bible, Copyright © 1983 by The Zondervan Corporation.

Scripture quotations marked NIV are taken from the Holy Bible, New
International Version®. NIV®. Copyright © 1973, 1978, 1984 by International
Bible Society. Used by permission of Zondervan. All rights reserved. [Biblica]

Scripture quotations marked RSV are taken from the Revised Standard Version of
the Bible, copyright © 1946, 1952, 1971 by the Division of Christian Education of
the National Council of the Churches of Christ in the USA. Used by permission.

Scripture quotations marked NASB are taken from the New American
Standard Bible®, Copyright © 1960, 1962, 1963, 1968, 1971, 1972, 1973,
1975, 1977, 1995 by The Lockman Foundation. Used by permission.

American Standard Version (ASV)
Public Domain

Contents

Chapter Four

Chapter Five

Chapter Six

Chapter Seven

Chapter Eight

Chapter Nine

Chapter Ten

Chapter Thirteen

Chapter Fourteen

Background Information

Who Are The True Jews Of The Bible?

ARE THE PURPORTED "AFRICAN-AMERICANS", Afro Americans, Black people of America truly descended from the indigenous individuals of Africa (Ethiopians, (Cush), Egyptians (Mizraim), Somolians, Libyans, South Africans)? No! They are the true Jews as indicated by the King James 1611 Version of the Holy Bible!

The Scriptures unmistakably depict the Jews of the Bible as having dark skin, or as you may say black skin.

Lamentations 4:8 says, "Their visage is blacker than a coal..." What is the meaning of the word "visage" in the dictionary? From The Concise Oxford English Dictionary, Tenth Edition (1999), "Visage" means – poetic/literary a person's face, with reference to the form of the features. A person's facial expression.

Realizing that the word visage relates to a person's facial highlights or features, if the Jews of the Bible have facial features darker than a coal, how are they Caucasian (Edomites)? Considerably all the more fascinating for what reason are their alleged white people alluding to themselves as Jews? Because the Devil is a Liar. The Edomites converted to our way of life in 135 BC and in 740 AD the people of Khazaria converted in the wake of mixing with Edomites that migrateded from Mount Seir to The Caucus Mountains, the genuine cave dwellers.

In Lamentations 5:10 we discover these words: "Our skin was black like an oven..."

In the event that the Jews of the Bible have skin "black like an oven", and this alluded to an even dark from sot, how are they Caucasian? Caucasian people can not whenever turn any shade of brown, they turn red! If they bath in the sun long enough that true shade of red comes out. You can not turn brown not to mention "black like an oven."

Caucasians lack melanin to even turn the lightest shade of brown. So now we have an issue. Somebody has been misleading the world and it has not been the "true Jews" but those convert lying Zionist fake Jews.

Job was an Israelite. We should perceive how he depicted himself. Take a look at Job 30:30:

"My skin is black upon me, and my bones are burnt with heat." Here, Job, an Israelite says his skin is black. At that point he says, "and my bones are burnt with heat", that is alluding to the tribulation that he was experiencing.

King Solomon, one of the wisest black men to ever walk the face of the earth, and probably the greatest king of the country of Israel, portrayed himself as a black man! In Song Of Solomon 1:1 it peruses, "The song of songs, which is Solomon's. I went to this verse to demonstrate this is Solomon speaking.

The world shows the falsehood this is some concubine or the Queen of Sheba speaking. I challenge anybody to approach and demonstrate as according to Scripture this is some "concubine" or "Queen of Sheba" speaking rather than Solomon himself.

Solomon, A Jew from the tribe of Judah, is portraying himself as black! Besides, here is the section in the Song of Solomon 1:5, "I am black, yet comely...;"

In the event that you look into the importance of the word for black, "shachar", as utilized in this section for evidence: This meaning of shachar from The New Strong's Exhaustive Concordance of the Bible (2003): 7838. Shachar from 7835; prop. dusky, yet in addition (absol.) jetty:- - black.

So "shachar" signifies "dusky". How about we turn that word upward and understand: The meaning of "dusky" from The Concise Oxford English Dictionary, Tenth Edition signifies "dusky" - adj. darkish in color.

So far brothers and sisters as indicated by the Scriptures:

1. Solomon portrayed himself as black in the Song of Solomon 1:5.
2. "Black" as used in Song of Solomon 1:5 in the antiquated Hebrew is characterized in The New Strong's Exhaustive Concordance of the Bible (generally viewed as one of the top concordances of the Bible) as "dusky"
3. "dusky" when characterized in a word reference in accordance with an individual being dark skinned!

If Solomon, a Jew from the tribe of Judah is depicting himself as dark skinned, how would he be able to or some other Jew written of in the Bible be white? Since the Devil is a Liar.

This isn't racism and charge Jehovah in light of the fact that those are his words through his messengers. Need to discover more data about the genuine character of the supposed African-Americans? Keep on reading!

As per Scripture, the Jews could never be white! The Bible reveals to you that Jacob (Israel), the forebear of the Twelve Tribes of the Nation of Israel, that "neither will his face presently wax pale". "Wax" is Old English which signifies "to turn". So to "wax pale" signifies to turn pale"... So if Jacob and his relatives' countenances would not "wax pale" which signifies "turn pale", by what method can a Caucasian be a Jew?

All Caucasian or alleged white people all through the world, regardless of whether they call themselves "American," "English," "Spanish", "French", "Jewish/Israeli", "Dutch", "German", etc..., are for the most part relatives of Esau, the mischievous more established brother of Jacob (Genesis 25:25, Malachi 1:1,2, Romans 9:13 KJV). You can be that way, comprehend that in all honesty. In any case, reality will go forward today. I censure you for the sake of Jesus.

The tribe of Judah from which the Jews of the Bible descend from are portrayed as "black" in the Bible! See Jeremiah 14:2, it portrays the tribe of Judah (the Jews) as being "black unto the ground," which means various shades of brown.

When you burrow through the ground, it is a wide range of shades of brown, from light brown colored to dark brown. You discover numerous shades brown (light brown to dark brown) among the supposed African-Americans.

The Lord said through the prophet Jeremiah that his legacy (Israel) is unto Him as a speckled bird in Jeremiah 12:9 KJV. A speckled bird has a wide range of colors. The Twelve Tribes of Israel are numerous shades of brown, Black, Hispanic and Native American. Tell it from the mountain, the true Jews are black and the Nation of Israel are those just referenced.

The oppression of the purported African-Americans is written in the Holy Bible and is a revile that relates to the Twelve Tribes of Israel!

If we kept the laws, commandments, resolutions and rules of our God, Jesus Christ, we would be honored and set high over all countries of the earth. (See Deuteronomy 28:15 KJV).

When you read from verses 15-68, the curses that befell the country of Israel just apply to the true Jews and Israelites (the people of Negro, Indian and Hispanic plunge dispersed all through North, South and Central America, the West Indies, Hispaniola, Puerto Rico, Cuba, and the four corners of the earth).

In any case, in accordance with the so-called African-Americans, the revile talked about in verse 68 unmistakably recognizes them as the true Jews. (See Deuteronomy 28:68).

One of the curses that came to pass for the true Jews is that they would be sent "into Egypt again with boats (ships)." "Egypt" isn't the genuine name of the African nation. The Egyptians called it "Kemet" in their local language of Kemau; the Israelites called it "Mizraim" in the Hebrew. "Egypt" additionally signifies "bondage" as indicated by Scripture:

(See Exodus 20:2 NIV).

So when the real dark skinned Jews were brought out of Egypt the first time, they were brought out of "a house of bondage." Read again Deuteronomy 28:68 NIV.

Again, when our people were brought out of Egypt (the African country), we were brought out of "a house of bondage." So Moses, a black man prophesized that the true authentic dark skinned Biblical Jews would go "into Egypt again" or a "house of bondage again. How? With ships!

What dark skinned people were brought into bondage with ships? Didn't this happen to the so-called "African Americans," "West Indians," and "Haitians"? Never this ever happen to the Caucasians who say they are Jews and are not! (Rev. 2:9 and 3:9 NIV).

Where it says "by the way thereof ye will be sold unto your adversaries (enemies) for bondsmen and bondswomen, and no man shall buy you." Where it says "and there" it implies the place we were taken into bondage by way of ships, which was America.

In that place, America, what does the Bible say would transpire? "...ye will be sold unto your enemies for bondmen and bondwomen." When we were brought here in servitude, we were in reality sold into subjugation by our adversaries (the white race) for bondsmen (slave men) and bondswomen (slave women).

Where it says "and no man shall buy you," that isn't stating we wouldn't be obtained, in light of the fact that now you as of now observe that we were sold unto our adversaries.

"Buy" written in the Older Quaker English the King James Version Bible is written in signifies "to save or to redeem." If you are redeeming somebody, you are saving them from evil. No man, be it Fredrick Douglas, Elijah Muhammad, Marcus Garvey, Malcolm X, Martin Luther King Jr., Al Sharpton, Louis Farrakhan, could save us from the evil that has and still is descending upon our people from 1619 to the present day with consistent mistreatment (oppression) by this nation America and the white race (Edom) on a wide range of levels.

The One in particular who can save us is Jesus Christ, by way of the God of Israel. As per the Holy Bible when Jesus walked among the Jews He likewise was Black (See Revelation 1:1, 14-15, Daniel 10:5,6 NIV).

The earliest paintings of Jesus accurately picture Him with a dark complexion. In any case, by the early Middle Ages, painters started painting Him with European highlights, for example, light skin, a bread, and long, light dark colored hair. In any case, As a Middle Easterner, Jesus in all likelihood would have been dark haired, with dark skin and Jewish.

From the beginning of time and in each culture, individuals would in general depict Jesus as somebody of their own race. Our Lord Jesus Christ, came to relate to people of each race (Matt. 28:17 KJV). God the Father loves all people and sent His Son to save the world (John 3:16,17; Rev. 5:9 KJV). That is Jesus Christ's mission and first priority!

More significant than distinguishing Jesus Christ's ethnicity is understanding His central goal - which included winding up some portion of humankind (John 1:14; Phil. 2:6, 7 RSV). In our current reality where race so regularly partitions people, Jesus Christ came to unite people in faith and love (John 13:34; Col. 1:14 KJV). God needs us to acknowledge each other in our differences (Gal. 3:28 NASB).

So, race and legacy fades away from plain sight when people from Jesus Christ's body expect their more shared way of life as the children of God with shared citizenship in heaven (Phil. 3:20 KJV). We can concur with the Apostle Paul, who stated, "There is neither Jew nor Gentile, neither slave nor free, nor is there male and female, for you are all one in Christ Jesus (Gal.3:28 KJV). In Christ the center mass of parcel has been separated. Jesus has a place with the whole world.

In the event that we could approach Jesus what race would he say he was for? His reverberating answer is - the whole human race. Jesus came to find, to seek and to save that which is lost. Those who Jesus Christ has saved, those who have accepted His salvation will be one day be reunited with Him in transformed bodies so that they will be like His glorious body (Phil. 3:21 RSV). Jesus not only predicted His death and resurrection, but also His ascension and exaltation (John 6:62; 17:1 KJV). His exit from life was as miraculous as His entrance. The account is given in Acts 1:9-11. Jesus Christ has now a position of power of glory (Eph. 1:20, 21, see also Heb. 6:20 ASV). He is now before God as our High Priest and Advocate (Heb. 9:24, 1 John 2:1 ASV). He has gone to prepare a place for us in heaven. He told his disciples "I will come back and receive you to be with Me that you also may be where I am" (John 14:3 NIV). Every Christian should look forward with deep anticipation to the return of his Lord for him. (See John 3:16-20 RSV).

Introduction

Oppression

OPPRESSION TAKES NUMEROUS FORMS - political, economical, and social - and the people of God are not spared its results (consequences). In the case of the Israelites, they endured 400 years under the Egyptians. This was especially difficult to take since God had promised Abraham that one day he would have a land that is his own.

God had likewise promised Abraham, "know about a surety that your relatives will be sojourners in a land that isn't theirs, and will be slaves there, and they will be abused for a long time" (Gen. 15:13 KJV).

The pattern of the Egyptian oppression of the Israelites is still with us today has practically vanished, in the feeling of the old routine with regards to purchasing and selling people, however there are a huge number of people whose lives add up to minimal more than slavery.

Political detainees suffer in numerous nations. Now and again, a large number of individuals are oppressed in labor camps. In Russia, for instance, those slaves include individuals condemned for damaging the nation's laws against spreading religion.

Be that as it may, when we consider oppression, we should not constrain ourselves to pondering the people who suffer under a Communist standard. A huge number of workers in Africa, Asia, and Latin America spend their lives at backbreaking work for a couple of pennies daily. In the ghettos of incalculable urban areas around the globe a large number of people are mistreated by neediness, appetite, and disease.

Legislative issues, financial matters, religion, and race are great powers that can be used to oppress individuals. In the United States we think that its difficult to appreciate this, except if maybe we are black, Indian, or Chicano.

The Christian over all others should be touchy to the individuals who suffer oppression. Christians are called upon to represent justice, to help lighten suffering, and to offer the good news of hope and harmony to all people. In this lesson we will find a portrayal of awful mistreatment, but also of the way in which Moses attempted to deliver his people.

Chapter One

The Egyptians Oppress The Israelites
(Exod. 1:7-14 KJV)

JACOB AND HIS SONS and their families originally came to Egypt, they got a warm welcome from Pharaoh, who said to Joseph, "Settle your father and your brothers in the best of the land" (Gen. 47:6 NIV). Jacob, obviously, had been dreadful about going to Egypt, despite the fact that the starvation (famine) in Canaan was serious.

In any case, the Lord said to Jacob, "Don't be afraid to go down to Egypt; for I will there make of you an great nation. I will go down with you to Egypt..." (Gen.46:3, 4 NIV).

It barely jumped out at anybody that God's plan for making an great nation out of Israel's relatives would include 400 years of mistreatment (oppression), however that is what occurred. This is another example of truth of Isaiah 55:8. "For my thoughts are not your thoughts, neither are your ways my ways, says the LORD." KJV

Barely any individuals are prepared for greatness if the cost is suffering, but frequently that is God's way. In these verses Moses, the writer of Exodus, gives us a blow-by- blow record of the Israelites' affliction (suffering).

The Israelites Prospered
(v. 7)

The book of Exodus starts with a short recorded synopsis that connections it with the events of the closing chapters of Genesis. The date of the Exodus from Egypt is by and large put at 1440 B.C., and since the bondage in Egypt kept going 400 years, the time of Jacob's entry in Egypt can be set around 1840 B.C. This verse gives a general picture of how the descendants of Israel (i.e., Jacob) prospered at the beginning of their visit in Egypt.

The fundamental picture is of an enormous population growth, material flourishing, and consequent influence ("became exceedingly strong"). This was in partial fulfillment of God's promise to Abraham (Gen. 17:2 KJV). In actuality, a new nation was growing inside the boundaries of an old and powerful nation.

"The land was filled up with them" alludes to "the place that is known as Goshen," which Pharaoh had given to Joseph's father and brothers

(Gen. 47:6 KJV). Goshen was a well-favored region fitted to flocks and herds. For reasons unknown the Egyptians hated shepherds (Gen. 46:34 KJV), and this is the reason the children of Jacob were put in this region, presumably the eastern delta of the Nile River.

They had some contact with the Egyptians (cf. Exod. 11:2, 3), however they were protected (shielded) from the plagues that God sent on the rest of the nation (cf. Exod. 8:22).

Pharaoh's Fear Of The Israelites
(vv. 8-10)

We don't know precisely to what extent this season of thriving kept going, but the impression is that a significant time frame passed under these conditions. Relations among Egyptians and Israelites without a doubt were well disposed, but abruptly the circumstance changed as a result of the rising of another king to the throne of Egypt.

It was not just that one king succeeded another. The ramifications of these realities ("there emerged another king...who didn't know Joseph") is that there was a difference in line (a change of dynasty). "Another king" is an expression not used elsewhere. This shows he didn't succeed his forerunner in common request of drop and legacy. he "arose" demonstrates that he occupied the position of royalty (occupied the throne) on various terms from the king whose place he took, either by usurpation or victory (conquest).

The way that he didn't know Joseph infers a total separation from the traditions of the nation. This man was neither familiar with Joseph, for not by any means mindful of his extraordinary and great services to Egypt. Hence, he cared little about Joseph's descendants.

In this way, he fundamentally changed the policies of the previous rulers toward the Israelites. Here we discover the rationale of reasoning for what was to end up serious mistreatment (oppression). Note the rationale of the ruler's discourse to his people. He initially engaged national pride by pointing out the growth and strength of the Israelites ("too numerous and too mighty for us").

This may have been actually valid, if the ruler contrasted the Israelites of Goshen and the number of inhabitants in the northeastern part of the nation after the shepherds were removed.

Dr. John Thomas Wylie

Next, the king referred to the risk to national security presented by the Israelites. They occupied outskirt (border territory) domain and it is insecure to have a wilderness frontier occupied by a foreign race. Their surrender to the adversary in case of an intrusion could be a definitive factor in war.

Apparently the ruler was not inventing this reason. Egypt's northeastern boondocks was pervaded with guerilla tribes. Western Asian countries frequently used these tribes to help assault Egypt, and the Egyptians shocked these attacks with impressive trouble.

Further, in language, highlights, dress, and in certain propensities the Israelites likely looked like those enemies of Egypt, so it was not out of request for the Egyptians to think about the Israelites probably similar to the characteristic partners of the trespassers.

The third purpose behind a difference in policy toward the Israelites is economic (financial): they may escape from the land. Here is the primary sign that the Israelites were thought of as an important wellspring of productive work. The new ruler is presently thinking about the conceivable loss of income and power, which would result from the withdrawal of this serene, innovative, industrious race of people.

The Forced Labor Plan
(vv. 11,12)

Pharaoh declared the need of dealing "shrewdly" with the Israelites. By this, he intended to devise a plan that would profit the Egyptians, paying little mind to the expense of the Israelites. It was anything but a plan that demonstrated any worry at all for the Israelites, who until this time had been loyal and faithful subjects.

Mistreatment (oppression) emerges when a more grounded party tries to exploit a more fragile (weaker) party for its own selfish ends. The more fragile one are thought of as non-essential for the objectives of the more grounded ones. The humanness of the mistreated or oppressed is ignored. They are considered basically as another material asset, not as human beings of respect, dignity and worth.

We normally think about the most noticeably awful sorts of persecution ever, for example, that suffered by the Jews in World War II, however abuse happens at whatever point any individual or people are misused, or used for narrow minded closures. This likewise occurred with the Afro-Americans in bondage. This can occur in the manufacturing plant, the workplace, at home, or at school. No, we don't call it abuse, however that is the thing that it is.

We "deal shrewdly" with individuals when we control (manipulate) them, cheat them, delude them, or damage their social equality in any capacity by discrimination. "We should keep them in their place," we sY about minority groups, "in case they get unreasonably strong for us."

To do that, we use their cheap labor for employments we believe are beneath us. This is a type of oppression that goes on in America, more than one hundred years after slavery was abolished.

Take a look at Pharaoh's cunning plan. He will take out two targets with one shot, in a manner of speaking. He would force slave work and power the Israelites to assemble two "store cities." This would shield the Israelites from heading toward the adversary (siding with the enemy) and simultaneously fortify the frontier. "Store cities" truly were towns for lodging weapons and supplies for defense and attack.

Pharaoh painstakingly organized this effort. "Task masters" were men of rank, administrators of public works. Under the task masters were overseers. The Israelites were divided into separations of laborers, every separation under a task master. Strictly speaking, they were not slaves.

Therefore, in spite of the fact that the burdens of building these urban communities (cities) were heavy, the Israelites kept on flourishing (they continued to prosper). They continued to occupy and cultivate their own district; they held ownership of their houses, flocks, herds, and other property.

They grew in numbers and strength, so their presence caused dread among their masters. "Dread" signifies a blend of loathing and caution (alarm). The Egyptians didn't respect and honor the Israelites for their boldness under constrained work (forced labor), but instead despised them for it.

Oppressors can't vanquish the spirits of mistreated (oppressed) people. There is a moral strength in the hearts of people that can't be overcome. Here, obviously, God was beginning to teach something to the Egyptians, so Pharaoh's plan backfired.

The Oppression Increased
(vv. 13,14)

Pharaoh concocted new plans of abuse (oppression) including constrained work, both in development and in field work. The world has never needed for malevolent plans to torment people.

History is filled up with ghastly instances of savagery and cruelty. People have become disposable to verify the objectives of dictators.

The Egyptians a lot prior has used merciless strategies to manufacture (build) the incredible pyramids. Presently we view them as marvels of the ancient world, but we seldom include the toll in human lives. So by the time of Israelites in Egypt there was an example of mistreating outsiders (foreigners) into this sort of building service.

There is a portrayal of brick-making in one of the old Egyptian temples. It shows prisoners (captives) under a general administrator, or task master, being driven to work harder by overseers armed with heavy whips. The supervisors shout out, "Work without fainting."

The Israelites likewise had to do "a wide range of work in the field." This included not just the farm work they were used to, but also burrowing channels and water system (irrigation) frameworks. Whatever the task, it was done under barbarous and harsh conditions.

Pharaoh's last technique was to control the Israelites by child slaughter (v. 16). Be that as it may, this appalling arrangement was likewise obstructed by God, who worked through the strong defiance of the Hebrew midwives (vv. 17-21). Here again we have a preview of God's final victory over Pharaoh, and of his ultimate care for the oppressed.

These are pitiful realities indeed, uncovering both the thought processes of the oppressor and the conditions of the oppressed. Every individual today needs to monitor his intentions in identifying with others. What's more, where oppression exists, much should be possible to enable the people who to suffer.

(How might you have felt as an Israelite as of now? Toward the Egyptians? Toward God? What

Dr. John Thomas Wylie

is oppression prone to do to people? Think about some individual or family you feel is oppressed. What might you be able to do to help them?

What are a few types of oppression you see around you? What thought processes in oppression would you be able to find? What fundamental spiritual needs are uncovered by oppression? In what capacity can these necessities be met by Christians with the good news of Jesus Christ?)

Chapter Two

The Impetuousness Of Moses
(Exod. 2:11-15a)

THE STORY OF MOSES begins with the faith and heroism of his mother (2:1-3). He was brought up as a child of Pharaoh's daughter. Moses himself disregards what occurred during his adolescence and youth, but the Bible lets us know (in the discourse of Stephen): "Moses was instructed in all the wisdom of the Egyptians, and he was mighty in his words and deeds" (Acts 7:22 RSV).

Later he settled on a cognizant choice to walk out on his Egyptian upbringing, "picking rather to share the evil treatment to the people of God than to appreciate the transitory pleasures of sin" (Heb. 11:25 NASB). In this passage from Exodus 2 we figure out how troublesome it was for him to distinguish himself with the abused and oppressed Israelites, who didn't comprehend his defense of one of them.

Moses Killed An Egyptian
(vv. 11,12)

In spite of the fact that Moses was brought up in Pharaoh's court, his genuine identity as a Hebrew was not kept from him. He likely had numerous chances to visit his home and family while he was growing up. On one of these events, when he was forty years of age (Acts 7:23), he went to visit his people and perceived how the Egyptians were oppressing them.

Clearly he knew about the forced labor camps before this, however on this day he came upon an Egyptian beating a Hebrew. The overseers were outfitted with long substantial, heavy whips and they practiced discipline by applying exorbitantly extreme, severe punishment with these whips. Moses was stirred by the sight. Exasperated by enthusiasm (patriotism) and empathy (compassion), he jumped into the brawl and slaughtered (killed) the Egyptian.

The overseer's beating more likely than not must have been cruel to excite the rage of Moses, yet this is no biblical support for murder. People under prolonged oppression frequently lash out in brutality or violence against their oppressors, yet there is no scriptural warrant for such reprisal. The Bible never defends Moses for this deed. He committed murder because He was provoked and as a result of his impetuous nature.

Obviously, Moses murdered the overseer also because he intended this to be a sign that he had totally broken with his Egyptian childhood so as to deliver his people from the Egyptians (Acts 7:25). He took things into his own hands and thus delayed their deliverance an additional forty years.

Moses' Deed Was Discovered
(vv. 13,14)

Moses figured he could shroud his deed by burying the person in question, but the following day brought a starling disclosure. He entered another squabble, this one between two of his own compatriots. When he attempted to isolate them and judge the man who began the fight, he was repelled. The man wouldn't acknowledge his mediation and cast up to Moses his murdering of the Egyptian. In this way Moses found that his deed was commonly known.

You can well envision that you had been the man delivered from the overseer's fierce whips, you would have announced the occasion far and wide. In a solitary day the news went all through the Israelite community. Additionally, Moses was a notable figure at this point among the Hebrews and the Egyptians.

Pharaoh Sought To Kill Him
(v. 15a)

Before long the whole nation caught wind of what Moses had done. Pharaoh, obviously, was angered. He took it as a treachery, a betrayal. Moses had been one of his own; presently he had chosen to agree with the loathed Hebrews. Along these lines, he chose that Moses himself had to go.

As per the laws of the time, no Egyptian ruler would have left such an offense unpunished, regardless of whether it had been submitted by a high-ranking Egyptian. Be that as it may, in light of the fact that Moses enjoyed the high position in Pharaoh's court, it was vital for the king to avoid potential risk. As a tyrannical over-lord, he was suspicious that Moses may lead the Hebrews in a rebellion.

So Moses needed to escape for his life. The Hebrews didn't identify with him, since they didn't comprehend that he was meaning to deliver them from the Egyptians. The recklessness of Moses revealed that he was not yet ready for the task of leadership. He had to learn meekness (Num. 12:3); he had to learn that "the anger of man doesn't work the righteousness of God" (James 1:20 KJV).

The people were to be delivered by God's power, not by Moses' strength. Moses had to learn the discipline of trust and obedience during an additional forty years as a humble shepherd.

(When you have been dealt with unjustifiably, how have you responded? What profound qualities may an individual learn under oppression? For what reason do you think Moses acted so thoughtlessly?

For what reason didn't the people comprehend his deed? What are a few ramifications for the abused when self-designated leaders do silly things? How might you offer thanks to God for freedom from abuse or oppression?)

Conclusion: Oppression is a reality that is awkward to confront on the grounds that it demonstrates the Bible's determination of the wickedness, and sinfulness of human beings.

The Bible alone represents abuse and oppression by revealing man's rebellion to God. The Bible likewise has the main solution for abuse and oppression: the person of Jesus Christ, who alone can deliver people from the power of sin that makes oppression and mistreatment break out.

Chapter Three

A Leader Called
(Exod. 3:1-12)

IN THE HUMAN PLAN of things leadership is a fundamental component. Without initiative there is disarray and perplexity. In God's dealings with his people, he additionally works through human leaders. Obviously, God could have coordinated individuals some other way, but in the Bible we learn how God quietly drove his people through various leaders.

The church as the noticeable institution for love and worship battles with the issue of leadership. In governmental issues, we choose leaders, in the military, they are advanced through the ranks; in education, they are chosen by scholarly fulfillment; in business, as per achievement in expanding benefits (profits). Every everyday issue has its own standards of initiative.

It is significant for Christians to get that despite the fact that God works through human leaders, he doesn't pursue human criteria in choosing them. The absolute least possibility for initiative were chosen by the Lord. From the viewpoint of achievement, the twelve apostles were not noteworthy according to the world.

Thusly, we see that in spite of the fact that God may choose an individual of bizarre ability and accomplishment to be his leader, similarly as regularly he may not. The reason is that God needs to show what he can do with individuals who probably don't have a lot to offer. That way, the glory and the praise go to God and not to any man.

Another reason behind why God's decision of a leader might be not quite the same as our decision is that "man looks on the outward appearance, but the LORD looks on the heart" (I Sam. 16:7 RSV). God alone knows the potential in an individual whose heart is directly toward him.

In this exercise today we perceive how God chose a shepherd in the wildness - Moses - to be the one to lead his people from bondage in Egypt. Moses had attempted to be a leader on his own terms; he fizzled and he failed, but God empowered him and enabled him to make a new beginning (a fresh start).

God Appeared To Moses
(Exod. 3:1-6)

Out of what seemed, by all accounts, to be absolute darkness and devastation, God started a point of contact with his suffering people. They had been in bondage in Egypt for a long time, but now God was going to accomplish something for them.

He started by revealing Himself to one man in an uncommon manner. These verses tell how gained the enthusiasm (the interest) of Moses through a wonderful miracle - a burning bush that wouldn't consume (was not devoured by its fire).

Moses Was A Shepherd
(v. 1)

In our past lesson we learned how Moses rashly attempted to expect a position of leadership for himself among the Israelites. He had gone to the defense of one of them and killed his Egyptian oppressor, but the Israelites repelled him. Pharaoh got some answers concerning the murder and Moses had to escape for his life.

Stephen reveals to us that Moses was forty years of age when he fled Egypt and that he lived as an outcast in the place where there is Midian for an additional forty years before God appeared to him (Acts 7:23, 30). Moses himself, the writer of Exodus, doesn't give us this sequence. Nor does he disclose to us anything about his frames of mind, his expectations, and his feelings of trepidation while he was shepherding for this father-in-law, Jethro. Moses had married Jethro's daughter Zipporah.

Be that as it may, following forty years of shepherding you can well envision that he may conceivably have surrendered any desire for coming back to Egypt and doing anything for his people there. However the writer of Hebrews says of Moses, "By faith he left Egypt, not being afraid of the anger of the king; for he endured as seeing him who is invisible" (11:27 KJV).

Therefore, we can be sure that Moses didn't surrender hope, even as the years delayed with no indication of God's intervention.

The experience of Moses in this circumstance should urge us to continue on in faith, when conditions appear to be dark and hopeless. Faith is the key to victory. God was with Moses even as a shepherd.

Dr. John Thomas Wylie

Moses was "on the shelf," in a manner of speaking, and evidently of no use to the Lord, yet that was not the part of the plan. Some way or another, Moses had soaked up so deeply at the foundation of faith that he was sustained during those four seemingly pointless decades.

One day Moses drove his sheep and goats to pasturage on the west side of the "wilderness," that is, the central zone of the landmass of Sinai. This was not an infertile waste, but a place with great field and water. It was around a three or four days' adventure from Midian, which was over the Gulf of Aqaba on the western edge of Arabia.

He came to Horeb, another name for Mount Sinai, in the southern part of the landmass. It is known as the "mountain of God" since it was where the glory of Jehovah was revealed to Moses, and furthermore where God gave the law to his people.

Moses Was Attracted To The Burning Bush
(vv. 2, 3)

While tending his flock Moses got a quick look at a peculiar thing: a desert bush was ablaze, but the branches weren't being devoured by the blazes. So he chose to investigate the marvel: "why the bush isn't burnt."

However, this was in excess of a curious fire or an exceptional bush. This was an appearance of "the angel of the Lord." When Moses took a look at a natural phenomenon, he recognized an intimation of the presence of God. This "angel" was not a winged creature, but God himself (v. 4).

This was not an immediate vision of God in bodily shape, be that as it may, for "nobody has ever seen God" (John 1:18). This was what Bible researchers call a "theophany," a form of God's self-manifestation. The "angel of the Lord" was now and again related to the Lord himself. There are, be that as it may, different occasions where the angel is distinct from the Lord.

In the Old Testament there is some diversity within the Godhead, which turns out to be all the more plainly found in the New Testament in the person of Christ and the Holy Spirit. As a matter of fact, in numerous appearances, "the angel of the Lord" is a foreshadowing of the presence of the second person of the Trinity, the Lord Jesus Christ.

For, as Old Testament scholar J. A. Motyer (2005) notes, "What other place in the Scripture is there One Who is indentical with the Lord but then distinct; Who, without deserting His deity, yet kept company with sinners; Who walked as a man among men; and Who, without denying the wrath of God, yet represent the supreme outreach of mercy?"

This symbolism of the burning bush is significant. It demonstrates that God is living (the bush was not consumed) and that he is holy (fire is the emblem of his purity). From this we see a picture of what God was to become to Moses. Commonly in later years these facts were to be the cornerstone of the authority (leadership) of Moses, whose supreme concern was the glory of God in his people.

Therefore, the burning Bush not only served to get the attention and interest of Moses, but also to teach him the essentials of his own knowledge of the living God.

God Spoke To Moses Out of The Bush (vv. 4-6)

God called Moses by name and Moses responded. At that point God gave Moses a indication of the holiness of the place and the event and identified himself as the God of the people of Israel. In effect, God was saying to Moses two things: (1) I am a holy God, and (2) I am your personal God.

Moses needed this self-authentication by the Lord. He had to be sure this was not a fantasy, a dream, or a hallucination. He could have been under the burden of heat; weird visions frequently occurred in the desert.

God cautioned Moses of the reverence that was due him as a result of his holiness. The spot itself was not holy; it just turned out to be holy at the presence and command of the Lord. Moses remained unaware of its holiness preceding this time, during forty years of shepherding.

Now God makes it holy and Moses should remove his shoes. This turned into a custom of worship in the temple and was all around followed in the East.

A keen sense of God's holiness is required for spiritual growth and leadership. True spiritual leadership springs from the respect, awe, and honor that are due God's name in light of who he is and what he is like.

Today a few leaders give the feeling (impression) that God is a major buddy, or pal in the sky. Moses never had that idea, and the New Testament cautions believers that "our God is a consuming fire" (Heb. 12:29 KJV).

God connected himself with the forefathers of Moses, Abraham, Isaac, and Jacob. Moses knew these men who had worshiped the one true God amidst surrounding paganism. Accordingly, this statement by the Lord was the connection Moses needed with his own people in Egypt.

Jesus cited this statement to demonstrate that the doctrine of the resurrection was taught in the Old Testament (cf. Mark 12:26). To him, these men served the God of the living, not the dead. For Moses, it more likely than not gave the idea that God was renewing his covenant of faithfulness to these men, for he had promised them that one day their posterity would enjoy a land of their own.

Moses responded with unsurprising fear; this was not a regular event. He shrouded his face in view of the acknowledgment that the was meeting God face to face. We can't envision what that resembled, however we can appreciate that appropriate response Moses made.

(How would you think Moses felt during those forty years of shepherding? Why? Have you at any point felt that God has forgotten you? Why? What should a Christian do when he feels like that? What are some unusual ways God has gotten your attention? How have you reacted? Aside from hearing the voice of God legitimately, in what capacity can Christians today get new motivations of God's holiness? What place would represent holy ground to you? Why?

God Called Moses
(Exod. 3:7-10 KJV)

The second step involved in God's calling of a leader is currently revealed. Moses is told of God's concern for the suffering of his people, and afterward he is given the staggering but overwhelming news that God wants him to lead the people out of Egypt.

The Affliction Of His
People Touched God
(vv. 7-9)

God was moved as a result of the cruelty of the treatment the Israelites were receiving from the

Egyptians. God told Moses, "I have seen...I have heard...and I have come down." It more likely than not appeared to the Israelites that God was cold-hearted, uncaring, that he was far removed from the terror of their condition.

This is the natural feeling when our deliverance from trouble isn't prompt. In any case, here we have the assurance that God cares; he sees our issues, hears our cries, and follows up for our sake (he acts on our behalf).

Obviously the Israelites didn't desert their faith in the Lord. They were crying unto the Lord, a reality that God rehashed to Moses. We do approach God through prayer, whatever our "taskmasters" may be, and paying little heed to the nature or degree of our abuse or oppression.

This is a troubling picture here of how the Israelites were mistreated, and God wanted Moses to know that he understood what the people were enduring. God said, "I know their sufferings." The articulation for "know" inplies a personal feeling, tenderness, and compassion.

Moses, the future leader, had to know not exclusively God's holiness and majesty, but in addition his lovingkindness and mercy. Without a doubt Moses more likely than not asked why

God didn't intercede to save his people from these terrible and awful conditions. Now he learns that God's heart was touched after all.

God likewise revealed to Moses that he was going to act: "I have come down to deliver them." It is one thing to express compassion, it is something else to act on behalf of the suffering.

These verses reveal to us that no persecution, no oppression gets away from the Lord; he see all the mischievousness of mistreatment today. In this way, we do well to share his compassion and follow up in the interest of the persecuted, the oppressed as he did.

God's deliverance included freedom from Egypt as well as a new homeland, "a land streaming with milk and honey." That land was now occupied by different tribes (v. 8), but God would make sure that the Israelites would have it for their own. Such is the graciousness of God. He acted out of his own unreservedly offered, freely given love, to show the suffering that he cared.

Knowing that God is like that helps us to endure issues today. We know he is holy and we are sinners, so we come to him for forgiveness; we know he is loving and compassionate, so we come to him for deliverance.

We come to God in prayer to find what his uplifting words of comfort and assurance are. Moses was given a preview of God's plan. We are not given a plan ahead of time of what is coming, but according to the New Testament we know that in Christ we lack nothing (cf. Eph. 1:3; Col. 2:10). Christ is God's love-plan of deliverance for us, regardless of what our abuse or oppression is.

He Wanted Moses To Lead
Them Out Of Egypt
(v. 10)

This announcement more likely than not come like a sensation to Moses. You can be certain that he was rejoicing over the news that finally God would take care of the suffering of his people.

In any case, how was God going to do this? This answer was: "I will send you to Pharaoh that you will bring forth my people...out of Egypt."

God's plans involves a human leader. Clearly, he could have acted otherwise; but he didn't. God's plan pursued the human method for getting things done. Each human organization has a leader. God's people at the time were leaderless; along these lines, Moses was given the responsibility.

It is important to comprehend this divine method; it follows right through the New Testament. It often has been said, "God's method is a person; consequently, what we need are better people." That is the key to spiritual leadership. Moses had to be disciplined more than forty years; that was rough training, but the immensity of the undertaking demanded a prepared leader.

There is no place in God's work where we can get by with messy or sloppy leadership. We ought to keep in mind the importance of our responsibility. Christians in like manner must be prepared to pay the price of spiritual preparation and training.

No one knows where or when God will open the door to a large responsibility and "call" some Christian to fill it. In any case, the facts show that if we are disregarding (neglecting) the responsibility we currently have, God won't give us a greater one.

What spiritual qualifications should a leader have? Did Moses have these? How would you know? In light of his experience here, how do you think Moses felt about God? Why? What should a person believe about God before he is prepared to accept responsibility? What must he believe about himself? In what sense is need-in this case, the suffering of the people-a factor in the call to Christian leadership?

Moses Was Reluctant To Accept
(Exod. 3:11, 12)

In these verses we find the first of Four reasons Moses gave as to why he was unfit for leadership: first in 3:11 and cf. 3:13-22 for the second; 4:1-9 for the third; and 4:10-17 for the fourth).

His First Objection
(v. 11)

His First objection (v. 11) From here through 4:17 we have a discussion between God and Moses about his hesitance to acknowledge the commission he had received. Moses' first reaction was basically, "Who am I?" Here is a totally unexpected frame of mind in comparison to the one reflected before when Moses wanted to assume leadership. Then he felt fearless, self-confident and capable for the task; now he considers himself nothing.

"Who am I?" demonstrate that forty years in the wilderness has been a humbling experience for Moses. He is never again the prince prepared to take control. Presently he believes that he is deficient for the task. However he has one characteristic of true leadership; humility. God's plan for his life has delivered this extraordinary quality to the degree that Moses is designated "submissive" or as the Scripture say, "very meek" (Num. 12:3 KJV).

Taking into account what he may suffer at the hands of Pharaoh, Moses could well have said that he was afraid to go, but his first dread is by all accounts his own incompetence, his dread of not having the option to carry out the responsibility (task) successfully. As of now Moses essentially figured he didn't have what it took to accept such a huge responsibility.

Second, God gave him a "sign," which for this situation implied a promise that rested totally on his word and demanded faith with respect to Moses. The promise that God would have his people serve him in that very place was an assurance to Moses, if he fully trusted it, that every single interceding hindrance would be removed by God's power.

So the potential leader is is cast completely upon the Lord, which is the vital nature of all evident true spiritual leaders.

Conclusion: How are leaders "called" today? The church must take a look at this basically as an issue of perceiving the hand of God on specific people, not as a prevalence challenge or as offering rewards to powerful individuals or enormous givers.

The church endures when spiritual qualities are not given priority; the church additionally suffers by disregarding or neglecting the preparation (and training) of leaders. Moses had a much to learn before he was ready to be God's leader.

Chapter Four

Let My People Go
(Exod. 11:1-6; 13:17-22)

AFTER 430 YEARS OF Bondage in Egypt, the Israelites were liberated (freed) by the Lord. There has never been another occasion very like it in the world's history. It is one of a kind on the grounds that for this situation a defenseless minority group gained its freedom from a superior power. Humanly, there was not the scarcest possibility that Israel could or would escape Egypt, but it occurred. Why?

Because God intervened and changed the oppressors' emotions by a progression of noteworthy supernatural occurrences (miracles), the alleged ten plagues on Egypt. After the tenth plague (the death of the first-borns sons) broke out, Pharaoh actually commanded the Isralites to leave. "Arise, go forth...serve the LORD....Take your flocks and your herds...and be gone; and bless me also! Pharaoh cried (Exod 12:31, 32 RSV).

Before this abrupt mass migration or exodus, Moses had demanded that Pharaoh free God's people, but Pharaoh had adamantly refused. He would not allow his supply of forced labor to be gone. The demand for freedom articulated by

Moses turned into a skirmish (a battle) of wills, as Pharaoh ardently opposed God's will.

Pharaoh's reaction to Moses' demand was rebellious or defiant: "Who is the LORD, that I should heed his voice and let Israel go? I do not know the LORD, and moreover I will not let Israel go" (Exod. 5:2 RSV). Along these lines, in securing freedom for his people God also forced the Egyptians to recognize his sovereignty.

God told Moses, "The Egyptians will know that I am the LORD, when I stretch forward my hand upon Egypt and bring out the people of Israel from among them" (Exod. 7:5).

As we study the details of the lesson here, we have to keep the basic issues firmly in mind: (1) God loved his people and responded to their abuse/oppression by giving them freedom, and (2) God proved to Israelites and Egyptians alike that he is the all-powerful leader of the universe who controls the destinies of men and nations.

The Last Plague
(Exod. 11:1-6 KJV)

In the earlier lesson we contemplated how God issued a call to Moses to deliver his people out of Egypt. In commissioning Moses for this assignment, God revealed to him that he would stretch out his hand and "smite Egypt with all of the wonders which I will do in it" (Exod. 3:20 KJV).

Moses was hesitant to acknowledge this call from the Lord (Exod. 4), but at last he obeyed and returned to Egypt, where his brother Aaron became his representative (his spokesman). When they revealed to the Israelites what God intended to accomplish for them, the people "bowed their heads and worshiped" (4:31 KJV).

Exodus 5-14 records the details of the battle among God and Pharaoh. Moses and Aaron, obviously, demanded freedom for the Israelites, however Pharaoh tirelessly would not concede it. After their first demand, Pharaoh only expanded the burdens on the brick-making Israelites (ch. 5). At that point God acted. Through Moses and Aaron he cautioned Pharaoh what he would do in the event that he neglected to release the Israelites.

(A point to remember is that God's people trust in his power for deliverance and guidance, even in what seems, by all accounts, to be hopeless conditions).

Water was turned to blood; frogs covered the land; "all the dust of the earth became gnats"; "great swarms of flies" came into the houses; "all the dairy cattle of the Egyptians died"; boils broke out on man and beast all through Egypt; "hail struck down everything that was in the field", locusts "ate all the plants in the land and all the fruit of the trees which the hail had left"; there was thick darkness in all the land of Egypt three days."

After the plagues of frogs, flies, hail, and locusts, Pharaoh relented, however, when the Lord removed these afflictions Pharaoh would not give the Israelites their freedom.

After the ninth plague (thick darkness) Pharaoh expelled Moses and cautioned him, "Get away from me;...never see my face again, for in the day you see my face you shall die" (10:28). Then God revealed to Moses what the tenth and final plague would be, and Moses in turn gave the warning to Pharaoh.

The Last Plague Will Be
The Turning Point
(v. 1)

When the Lord had called Moses, he said, "See that you do before Pharaoh every one (all) of the miracles which I have put in your power" (Exod. 4:21 KJV). In any case, Moses didn't have the foggiest idea what number of various diseases he would call downward on the Egyptians. Presumably, he was thinking about what it would take to change Pharaoh's attitude.

Along these lines, God revealed to him (told him) this would be the last plague, at that point Pharaoh would relent. Pharaoh would not just allow authorization for the Israelites to leave, he likewise would drive them out of Egypt. He would after one more sign from the Lord give up (surrender) his will to God's will.

All through this record the issue is the hardness of Pharaoh's heart. God had revealed to Moses that Pharaoh would not let the Israelites go "unless compelled by a mighty hand" (Exod. 3:19 KJV). Now and again during the plagues, the record says that Pharaoh hardened his heart; at different occasions, it says that the Lord hardened his heart. When God called Moses, he warned him, "I will harden his (Pharaoh's) heart, so he will not let the people go" (4:21 KJV).

Here is where it pleased God to reveal early how Pharaoh would respond to the plagues.

As opposed to subdue his heart - as disasters sometimes do - they would harden it. The effects of God's judgments, being foreknown, are willed by him.

The hardening of Pharaoh's heart, while it might appear to be cruel to us, was a part of God's judgment on him. In one sense, Pharaoh hardened his own heart as a result of his consequence of his basic attitude: "Who is the LORD, that I should heed his voice?" On the other hand, it is likewise correct to say that God hardened his heart as a righteous judgment on him, in light of his persecution (oppression) and brutalities.

Truth be told, God explained that the plagues were without a doubt "great acts of judgment" (6:6; 7:4 KJV). The motivation behind why God revealed what he was doing to Pharaoh was to sustain the spirit of Moses and the people during the process of events. They were taught that both the plagues and the obstinence of Pharaoh were altogether foreseen and predetermined by God.

Yet God was eminently reasonable (fair) with Pharaoh. As has been said, "The sun by the activity of heat makes wax moist and mud dry, hardening the one while it softens the other; by the same activity producing exactly opposite results. Thus from the longsuffering of God some derive benefit and others harm, some are softened while others are hardened."

Neighbors Would Relinquish Their Jewelry To The Israelites
(vv. 2, 3a)

After four centuries of bondage the Jews had aggregated nearly nothing, assuming any, riches. As of late they had works as brickmakers; they were slave workers. Presently they were going to leave on an overland journey with little of this present world's goods, however God had a plan to accommodate their needs.

They were to approach their Egyptian neighbors for silver and gold. At this point the Israelites were dissipated all through Egypt, never again kept to Goshen. What a bold activity!

How could slaves ask masters for jewels? By one way or another, defeating their hesitance, the Israelites did this. You can envision their anxiety when moving toward the Egyptians. All things considered, God moved the Egyptians to give away their silver and gold (cf. 12:36). This in itself must be considered a miracle.

By this plan God achieved two things: (1) His people didn't leave Egypt with practically nothing, and (2) the Egyptians were "pillaged, despoiled." Out of his judgment upon Egypt came God's plan for his people. This peculiar technique had been revealed earlier to Moses (cf. 3:21, 22 KJV).

Moses Gained In Stature
(v. 3b)

Here is an summary of how God gave the leader of his people a great standing among the Egyptians. Once more, this is startling, in light of the fact that leaders of exploited people are not commonly appreciated by the exploiters.

If we find that its difficult to understand how the people of Israel gained favor with the Egyptians, it is considerably progressively hard to get a handle on how they regarded Moses. God was at work changing attitudes.

The people knew that Moses was the one humanly in charge of the plagues that caused such extraordinary hardship and obliteration (destruction). Should they not hate him? However, Moses also brought each plague to and end, offering relief to the people. In advance of the plagues he gave warnings and attempted in certain examples to spare them suffering (cf. 9:19, 20 KJV).

The greatness of Moses according to the people without a doubt was related with his powers, which they thought were his own. They don't knew anything about the fact that he was so reluctant to assume leadership. They didn't know that Moses was God's instrument. However, it was a part of God's plan of deliverance to use a man like Moses and to exalt him according to (in the eyes of) the Egyptians.

All The First-Born Will Die
(vv. 4-6)

The words of Moses to Pharaoh ought to be read following he last verse of chapter 10. Moses didn't leave the presence of Pharaoh until after he revealed to him what God's next step would be. At that point he withdrew furiously (angrily) (v. 8) and the last interview with Pharaoh was finished.

The last judgment was the most horrendous (the most dreadful). In each Egyptian family, from the greatest to the least, the first-born would die. The cows were included. The outcome would be the most awful distressing the nation had ever or could ever experience.

The tenth plague was unmistakable in character from all the others; it was the solitary one that brought death home to the Egyptians. Most significant, it would achieve the deliverance of Israel.

God's judgment on Egypt's first-born was also revenge for the Egyptians' executing of all the male children of the Israelites. The people as well as Pharaoh had participated in this child murder (Exod. 1:22 RSV). The judgment on the cattle is identified with the Egyptians' worship of animals. Each home had its very own sacred animal.

We don't realize precisely how long mediated between the warning and the execution of this judgment (12:29, 30), but it more likely than not been a few days so the Israelites could get ready for the Passover and depart from Egypt. Meanwhile, the Egyptians lived under the shadow of this menace.

(How would you think Moses felt during the time of the plagues? Why? How might you have felt as an Israelite? Why? As an Egyptian? How does Pharaoh outline the risk of an unyielding demeanor toward the Lord? How is resistance (rebellion) to God showed today?

What are a portion of the consequences? How are people misused today by the people who won't accept God's sovereignty? What would Christians be able to do to protect their faith and maintain hope in God's loving plan?)

The Exit From Egypt
(Exod. 13:17-22 KJV)

Moses trained the Israelites in God's plan for saving them from the plague of death on the first-born youngsters and cattle. The blood of a sheep, spread on the doorposts and the lintel of the houses, was an indication to the Lord, who said, "When I see the blood, I will pass over you" (12:13 KJV). Simultaneously, the observance of the ceremony of the Passover was established.

Then, when the Lord destroyed every one of the firs-born of Egypt, the people rose up "to send the Israelites out of the land with haste" (12:33 KJV). The verses from chapter 13 depict the beginning of the Exodus from Egypt.

God's people had obeyed with his commands unequivocally. Everything occurred as Moses had said it would.

The first-born in Israel were saved, the passover meal was eaten "in haste," and after that the people departed rapidly. They had eaten with their "lions girded, "sandals on their feet, and staffs in their hands. They took the Egyptians' jewelry and clothing, but nothing else aside from unleavened dough and their cattle (cf. 12:33-39 KJV).

Not By Way Of The Philistines
(v. 17)

The company of the Israelites numbered "around 600,000 men by walking, other than women and children" (12:37 KJV), so the all out came to almost 2,000,000 people. How this mass movement was done amazes the creative mind.

In any case, we should recall that during the year of the plagues Moses had trained the people on the most proficient method to compose themselves for the Exodus. After the primary plague the Israelites most likely regathered and started to think about their numbers and assets.

Three times after that Pharaoh had given restrictive consent (conditional permission) for the Israelites to depart. Those were the in all probability times Moses gave instructions for the march.

The first stop was Succoth (12:37), most likely the base camp (headquarters) town of the Jews in Goshen and where Joseph's bones were kept. Instead of movement northeastward along the Mediterranean coast to Canaan, by a nearly short course, the Israelites were coordinated another way. The reason behind the diverse course was the presence of the warlike Philistines along the coast, in the region currently known as the Gaza Strip.

Inevitably, the Israelites would have to fight, but the Lord knew they could be discouraged or demoralized by a fight so soon after their leaving Egypt.

By Way Of The Wilderness
(v. 18)

The route shown by the Lord in the long run took the Israelites southward toward Sinai. It is hard to recognize the course precisely with present day topography (and modern geography). Place names change thus does the geology. (Counsel a Bible atlas chart book for the different potential courses.)

What this implied was the crossing of the Red Sea (not to be mistaken for the waterway presently known as the Red Sea), or "Reed Sea" or "Marsh Sea," an old lake or gulf situated along what is currently the Suez Canal.

The Israelites were eqiipped for battle. "Having occupied a frontier region that was the area of continuous attacks by travelers (nomads) and guerillas, they were acquainted with the use of arms. There is no sign that they had been incapacitated by the Egyptians. Actually, Pharaoh expected that they may one day join invaders against Egypt (1:10).

"Equipped" has been made translated also to signify "marshaled in a systematic exhibit (orderly array)." This may suit the setting better, in light of the fact that there is no proof to recommend that the Israelites were a strong military force.

Moses Took The Bones Of Joseph
(v. 19)

The request of Joseph - made in faith that God would bring the descendants of Israel into their own land (Gen. 50:24, 25) - was handed down through the generations. Moses knew about it and ensured that it was done.

God Led Them By Cloud And Fire
(vv. 20-22)

The Israelites clearly were efficient, well organized. There is no real way to represent this mass movement apart from superb organization and discipline. Perhaps they learned this in Egypt. Much of it was taught by Moses. However there was more than human ingenuity involved here.

God gave them his very own divine guidance as a cloud by day and a fire by night. This was the assurance of his presence and security (protection). It additionally enabled them to travel at night through an obscure territory.

Moses was a wise, skillful leader, obviously, but he was subject to God's direction. He was receptive to the voice of the Lord, and didn't map out his very own getaway (escape) route. He, as well, was subject to these signs of God's direction.

These outward symbols of God's blessing stayed with the Israelites all through their forty years of wandering in the wilderness, despite their sin and unbelief (cf. Neh. 9:18, 19).

(For what reason do you think God didn't lead the Israelites by the brevity course to Canaan? What sorts of preparation - physical and spiritual - did the Israelites have to make for the Exodus? What was required of them to escape from the plague of death on the first-born?

For what reason was the passover established as a statute forever in Israel? What was it intended to symbolize? For what reason do you think they needed a pillar of cloud and fire to lead them? How are God's people led today?)

Conclusion: The Exodus from Egypt is remembered today as the high point of Israel's history. In the Old Testament, the prophets admonished Israel to go back to God based on his redeeming grace in delivering them from bondage. For them, the Exodus was ever to be remembered with gratitude and obedience.

In the New Testament, Jesus Christ is pictured as accomplishing the final "exodus," that is, the Christian's full redemption. In this sense, Egypt represents bondage to sin. God's power in delivering ancient Israel is accessible today to deliver people from the power of sin.

Christians today live on the opposite side of the "mass movement or the exodus" in a manner of speaking. "Let My People Go" today is a cry for freedom from bondage to sin. By faith anybody can reach out and get freedom from sin, because Jesus Christ died and rose again.

Similarly as the Israelites were encouraged to look to the Exodus from Egypt as the basis of their worship and service to God, so the Christian today thinks back to the cross of Jesus Christ for his inspiration and motivation.

Chapter Five

The Celebration Of Freedom
(Exod. 14:21-25, 30, 31; 15:1-3)

CELEBRATION IS A WORD we don't regularly associate with the church. You may think about a Fourth of July celebration, or a birthday or commemoration celebration, but by one way or another in our way of life celebration and worship don't go together.

Many Christians have come to acknowledge the hour of worship as a period of calm reflection and supplication, when they tune in to a sermon, sing a few songs, and recount responsive readings. When much else vivacious and emotional is presented, they state it isn't fitting for worship.

So in spite of the fact that we partner celebration with functions and festivities of one kind and another, we have not enabled ourselves to express our Christian faith similarly. However our statement commend originates from a Latin word that was used of solemn services.

That is the reason our Roman Catholic brothers and sisters discuss celebrating the Mass. Simply, to celebrate intends to watch a day or honor an occasion. There is no motivation behind why Christians can't celebrate what God has accomplished for them. Maybe if we celebrate all the more straightforwardly, the people who think church is stuffy would be attracted to worship.

Happiness and bliss should mark the meeting up of Christians. They are the beneficiaries of the best endowment of all, salvation in Jesus Christ. They have a great deal to cheer about, to rejoice about, to celebrate about, more than other people do.

This lesson shows how the Israelites celebrated their freedom from Egypt. Their celebrating sets the example for all believers. The Bible doesn't present one custom for worship, but the Bible reveals that God's people ought to celebrate what he has accomplished for them.

Deliverance From The Egyptians (Exod. 14:21-25 KJV) (PROOFREAD)

Israel's break from Egypt was not without its frightening, terrifying experience. When "the Lord smote all the first-born in the land of Egypt" (12:29 KJV), the Egyptians responded in a furor and asked the Israelites to leave in haste.

Be that as it may, God was not yet through with Pharaoh and his compatriots (countrymen). Pharaoh had bragged before Moses and Aaron that the God of Israel was nothing to him, and God promised to Moses that one day Pharaoh would acknowledge him.

God was doing two things: allowing freedom from bondage and persecution to his people, and showing Egypt and the nations who was really the supreme leader of the world.

Be that as it may, this teaching part of the Exodus was not yet completed. God took his people through the nerve racking Red Sea experience "to get glory over Pharaoh and all his host" (14:4 KJV). At that point the Egyptians would know that God was the Lord.

Obviously, the Israelites learned something about their God, as well. They froze (panicked) when the Egyptians sought after them; they grumbled to Moses and said it would have been better to die in Egypt (14:10-12 KJV). Be that as it may, Moses told them to overcome their feelings of dread, to stand firm, and God would deliver them.

The route out of Egypt more likely than not appeared to be a convoluted bypass (tortuous detour) to the Israelites (13:18; 14:1, 2 KJV). Be that as it may, even reroutes, harsh as they may be, can be learning encounters in our walk with God. In the event that we follow him into what seem like alternate routes, we can trust in him to show us something and to bring glory to himself.

The Israelites Crossed On Dry Ground (vv. 21, 22)

The scene is the northeast corner of Egypt between the Gulf of Suez and the Mediterranean Sea. (The Red Sea of current geology isn't the Red Sea of this episode). The term Red Sea (13:18) signifies "sea of reeds" or "weeds." Moses tells the towns it was near (14:1, 2 KJV). This is known as the Bitter Lakes region of Egypt, generally between Qantara (thirty miles of Port Said) and just north of Suez.

Pharaoh, understanding that his stockpile (supply) of forced workers was leaving, sought after the Israelites with a relentless armed force (14:5-9). Be that as it may, God secured the scared Israelites by bringing the pillar of cloud among them and the Egyptian army.

The Israelites, caught between the Egyptians and the Red Sea, were advised to "go ahead" (14:15 KJV). God had told Moses when he got to the water, and how he would enable his people to cross on dry land and crush the Egyptians (vv. 16-18).

In this way, when Moses got to the Red Sea, he did as God had commanded. While he put out his hand over the water, God drove a path through the water by means of a strong east wind that blew throughout the night. The outcome: "the waters were divided" and the people crossed the sea on dry ground.

The rod that Moses held out over the water was emblematic of God's leading and the authority he had committed on Moses. The people without a doubt had gained from past experiences what the rod represented, but this crossing was as yet an enormous test of their faith and obedience.

They had been incapacitated by fear and complaining, but now they obeyed the command of God through Moses. Moses and Aaron most likely took the first steps onto the sand between the treacherous walls of water transcending on either side of them.

The people were encouraged to follow, but you can be certain they did as such with extraordinary fear, wondering if at any moment the water may overwhelm (engulf) them.

In any case, God's power didn't come up short (did not fail); he was faithful to his promise. He used a natural agent, the east wind, to achieve powerful supernatural results.

The Egyptians Were Overcome
(vv. 23-25)

Presumably the Egyptians – leaving out of the cloud - didn't know precisely where they were, so they plunged quickly after the Israelites. Pharaoh would regularly be the leader of his soldiers, which for this situation were mounted on steeds and chariots.

From a human angle, it resembled a simple triumph for the Egyptians. The Israelites not exclusively were mediocre militarily, but additionally they were eased back by the huge large number of men, women, and children - young and old the same - walking with every one of their assets.

Be that as it may, abruptly the picture changed. God again intervened and caused massive equipment failure and perplexity among the Egyptians. We are not told by what means God did this, albeit some think there was a blaze of light from out of the pillar of the cloud that made the steeds jolt. Whatever the means, the Egyptian chariots ran together and were not able proceed with the pursuit.

The Egyptians themselves perceived the hand of God in this. They couldn't represent the unexpected breakdown in military order. The mayhem was extraordinary to such an extent that the positions were broken and they chose to escape. This was probably the best turnaround in military history, if not the best.

God had anticipated, "The Egyptians shall know that I am the LORD," and in this tumult the Egyptians recognized the power of God. Their only thought however was by one way or another to get away. They had officially numerous striking experiences of God's staggering and devastating power in their land. Regardless of how mortifying it may be to escape before Israel, the Egyptians chose to turn and run, however it was past the point of no return (it was too late).

Pharaoh and his military perished when the waters continued their regular levels at the direction of Moses under the command of God. So it was that God achieved an undisturbed march for his people through territory subject to Egypt and its military power.

The loss of thousands of men and Pharaoh himself was not fatal to Egypt, however historians disclose to us that Egypt was not ready to mount another expedition into this territory for another seventeen years.

The Red Sea crossing was simultaneously God's ultimate judgment on Egypt and his irreversible deliverance of Israel. It carried his people to a sense of national-consciousness that was really spiritual.

The crossing was exceptional to such an extent that it was always remembered as a reality (fact), in spite of the fact that the demands of the covenant on which it was based frequently were.

This powerful and mighty miracle was viewed as indisputable verification of God's love and the just basis of his claim to the devotion and obedience of his people. All through the Psalms it is celebrated as a significant event in Israel's history (cf. Ps. 66:6;74:13; 106:9; 136:13). In the New Testament, the crossing is cited as an example of the faith of God's people (Heb. 11:29 KJV).

(How might you have felt as an Israelite caught between the Egyptians and the Red Sea? For what reason do you think some about the people would have wanted to remain slaves in Egypt? For what reason do you think Pharaoh chose to seek after the Israelites, even after the death of the first-born in Egypt? How people today discover who the Lord truly is? In what conditions throughout your life have you seen God get glory to himself?)

Rejoicing For Deliverance
(Exod. 14:30, 31; 15:1-3 KJV)

Israel's life as a nation started on the east side of the Red Sea. The people at last were isolated from the idolatry of Egypt. Starting now and into the foreseeable future they would be distinguished as the people of God. The encompassing nations would know them as the people whom Jehovah had phenomenally miraculously freed from Egypt (Josh. 2:10 KJV).

In any case, before the journey to the promised land at Canaan began, the Israelites participated in a tremendous victory celebration.

For this situation, in any case, God himself was honored. It was his victory and the glory belonged to him. Time and again, when people are diverted by the spirit of the moment from everything else, they neglect to express gratefulness to God.

Christians can serve a significant job by reminding others the amount we owe to God. The principle of honoring God initially applies to family, community, and national celebrations.

The People Trusted God
(vv. 30, 31)

What an awesome sight it more likely than not been to see the bodies of the Egyptian cavalrymen washed up on the shore of the sea. These officers spoke to the power of Egypt that had held Israel in bondage for a long time (430 years). Now they were bodies on the sand - not on the grounds that the Israelites had killed them, but because God himself had intervened.

The central certainty of history is that "the Lord saved Israel," Israel didn't save herself. So it must be with every one of our blessings: God gives them to us, he saves us. Nobody is entitled to celebrate as a result of what he himself has done. All glory belongs to God. There is nothing we can do to win our salvation. God alone saves; he vanquished or conquered sin and death in the person of his Son, Jesus Christ.

The people looked at the Red Sea and saw what God had done to Egypt. Christians today can take a look at the cross of Calvary and see what God did to secure their salvation. Jesus suffered death so we may be free from the bondage of sin.

God did a "great work" against the Egyptians, so the people feared him and had confidence (faith) in him and in Moses. Obviously, they would feel overwhelmed by the compelling power of God so clearly exhibited before them.

Theirs was a legitimate proper response. This healthy dread drove them to a position of trust in God and in Moses. They needed to commit to God and to their leader at the beginning of their walk to Canaan.

Confidence (faith) in God was needed in view of the extraordinary dangers that anticipated them. In any case, they likewise expected to trust in their leader, for the sake of organization and unity, in case there be insubordination, rebellion and confusion in the ranks.

Later on, when the open door came to enter Canaan, the people lost their confidence (faith) in God, and during the forty years of wandering in the wilderness there was consistent dispute among them. Now at this point of magnificent and glorious victory, be that as it may, the people made glad allegiance to God and to Moses.

The Victory Of The Lord
(v. 1)

The celebration began with a hymn. It was composed on the spot by Moses himself. Here we have the start of music as a focal part of worship. This was to be the example for the Jews and the Christians.

Today our hymns look back to what God accomplished in Christ, but even here in this dramatic hymn we discover much that we can sing about.

(The hymn is in three sections: vv. 1-5, an ascription of praise to God and a concise picture of what had just occurred; vv. 6-10, a more detailed description of the crossing, including the attitude of the Egyptians; vv. 11-18, more praise to God and a prediction of future triumphs.

Their deliverance from Egypt was the token of a complete fulfillment of old promises. It was likewise a pledge that enemies to be encountered in the future on would be overcome and that Israel would gain the inheritance of Abraham).

The celebration of worship is directed to the Lord, not to man. It was God who had "triumphed gloriously"; it was God who had tossed the Egyptian warriors and steeds into the sea. Therefore, the praise must be given to him. The literal Hebrew in this implies God is gloriously glorious.

Moses knew that the hearts of people can be moved in praise by singing together. Clearly, the people had no background for this, so Moses must be the song leader as well as the composer. But once this sublime poetry was learned, a mighty crescendo of praise arose to God.

His words capture the spirit of what had just occurred. When we worship, we should find ways to express what God has accomplished for us. Music in worship isn't for entertainment, however for the expression of our true feelings about God.

The Strength Of The Lord
(v. 2a)

Singing to the Lord means disclosing to him how great he is. Most celebrations revolve around characters: military legends, political champs, and victors in games. We join the celebration to demonstrate appreciation. So it is in the celebration of Christians.

The Israelites observed God's strength and his salvation. They had seen power and deliverance; no big surprise he was their song. Here is a testimony that any Christian can give.

This testimony should be the heart of our worship celebrations. Each time believers gather they can celebrate God's strength and salvation. Christians have not seen the Egyptians pulverized by God, however they have seen his power in their lives.

Then again, one explanation maybe that Christian worship often is devoid of victory celebrations that the worshipers have lost sight of what God has accomplished for them. They discover little to celebrate about. Except if we walk close to God by prayer and Bible reading, we can lose the excitement of God's triumphs on our behalf.

The Praises Of The Lord
(vv. 2B, 3)

"Praise" signifies to celebrate with appreciative, cherishing reverence. That is the heart of worshiping with "spiritual freedom." This implies more than feeling or emotion. We worship with our minds just as well as our hearts.

"I will praise him...I will exalt him" is the promise made by the rejoicing Israelites. They celebrated the goodness of the Lord. Christians today exercise the same discipline. Worship doesn't occur consequently in light of the fact that it happens to be Sunday. The Christian must be moved by a true, genuine experience with Jesus Christ.

If worship seems less than celebration, it may be on the grounds that those in participation have not had a striking, vital crisp walk with God. Worship can't be vital if it is done out of routine or habit. "This is my God" speaks of spiritual personal experience.

Since the Israelites had seen God at work vanquishing their adversary, they called him "a man of war." This was how he acted on their behalf; this was not a description of his character.

God spoke to their immediate needs in a wartime situation.

God inspires our praise today in a variety of circumstances. If we are attentive (observant), we can find reasons to celebrate God's goodness and benevolence (mercy) in each experience of life.

In every time of Christian victory lyricists have been inspired to celebrate God. In the book of Revelation (15:3) this song of Moses is connected with the final triumph of Christians, when believers "with harps of God in their hands" will sing "the song of Moses...and the song of the Lamb."

(In what experiences with Christ have you felt unique (special) inspiration? How did you express your praise? Have you ever written your praise to God? What elements of God's work on your behalf would you like to celebrate? Do you believe God's victory in "Jesus Christ is the central point of worship in your church?)

While we for the most part praise God for his blessings, it is good to think about specific incidents in our walk with God. If our goal is to celebrate God's deliverance, then we shall be alert every day to see his hand guiding us.

The Christian need not trust that seasons of emergency or crisis to celebrate. He should cultivate the discipline of mind and heart to praise and exalt the Lord continually.

Chapter Six

Called Into Covenant
(Exod. 19:2-9; Deu. 11:8, 9, 18, 19)

WHEN OFFICIAL BIBLE READING and prayers were prohibited from the government funded educational systems by the Supreme Court (roughly 1962, 1963), many individuals felt it was a serious misfortune to our children. Educators who needed to take care of business felt their options were limited (their hands were tied). In any case, continuously throughout the years another methodology (a new approach developed) developed.

In many secondary schools and universities, the Bible was being educated by and by. Genuine, however it was not being instructed as the authoritative Word of God in the Christian sense, but it was being taught as a great literature. Truth be told, Bible courses had become one of three regions of most prominent demand in secondary school literature courses.

Indeed, even this approach has it value, since it exposes young people to the great biblical topics of redemption, providence, and judgment. The exciting story of Israel's deliverance from Egypt, which we contemplated earlier, is a feature of biblical literature. Furthermore, obviously another noteworthy event is the inauguration of God's special relationship with the people of Israel, the subject of this lesson.

These two events make legitimate subjects for study in church and schools alike, because they deal with such important issues. When a person looks at the Bible even as great literature, he finds himself meeting the God who wants to be personal. When God gave his commands to his people, there were no schools to show them, so God gave that duty to parents.

We can be appreciative that a few schools (private or theological schools) are studying the Bible, however we ought to always remember what God expects of parents. Children ought to learn of God as a matter of first importance in the circle of "the family" Bible reading and prayer. This is a responsibility or duty regarding what Christian parents should do.

God's Plan For His People
(Exod. 19:2-9)

After their victory celebration, the people of Israel began the burdensome trek to Canaan (follow the course on a Bible map). It wasn't long before trouble developed on the grounds that the people whined and complained about the lack of food, so God provided quail and manna.

Then the people got parched (thirsty) and whined, complained to Moses once more, and God gave them water out of a rock. Next, the individuals of Amalek battled against Israel, but Israel won. At long last, following three months, the Israelites came to Sinai, where God described his special plans for them.

Encamped At Sanai
(v. 2)

As God had promised Moses (Exod. 3:12 KJV), he brought the people to Mount Sinai ("the mountain," also known as Horeb). The wilderness of Sinai is situated between the Gulf of Suez and the Gulf of Aqaba.

The peninsula itself is generally a wild, ungracious territory (hospitable) supporting little life. It is a elevated tableland standing somewhere in the range of 2,000 and 2,500 feet high. There is a marked lack of water in the region, and even the Wadi el Arish, the "River of Egypt," is dry for the greater part of the year.

The location of Mount Sinai itself has involved impressive debate. Four different mountains have been supported by scholars over the years. Two specifically have strong support: Jebel Musa and Ras es-safsafeh. The former has the support of ancient tradition going back to the fourth century, while the latter appears to be a better choice in view of a large plain at its foot that could have accommodated the encamped Israelites.

What God Had Done
(vv. 3, 4)

This encampment was to last the better part of a year. The people moved when the pillar of cloud and fire moved; else, they stayed in camp. Here Moses began to go about as go-between among God and the people when God revealed his special covenant relationship with them.

As Moses ascended the mountain, he heard the voice of the Lord. God disclosed to him what to say "to the house of Jacob...the people of Israel. "Israel, obviously, was the name God had given to Jacob after the all-night wrestling match. The name was given to him since he had strived with God and with men, and had prevailed (Gen. 32:22-32).

This is the only place in the five books of Moses where God uses the articulation "house of Jacob" to depict the new nation created by deliverance from Egypt. It is used fittingly at this critical point since it helps Moses to remember the special promises made to Jacob.

The primary concern here is strikingly clear: before God's covenant with his people can be revealed, they should look back once more at recent events. God calls the people as witnesses of what he had quite recently accomplished for them in safeguarding them from bondage in Egypt. They couldn't deny what they had seen.

Three articulations outline their ongoing experiences: what God had done to the Egyptians; how God had borne them "on eagles' wings"; and how he had brought them to himself. The whole experience of deliverance is flawlessly and beautifully wrapped up in the expression, "how I bore you on eagles' wings."

Both in the Old Testament and in the New God's people are compared to fledglings which the mother cherishes and secures under the wings. In the Old Testament, that mother is an eagle; in the New, a hen. The image of the eagle speaks about God's power which he demonstrated when he brought the people out of Egypt with a strong hand and an outstretched arm, and led them into the Promised Land.

The picture of the hen, used by Jesus, pictures his coming in humility to take the form of a servant and become obedient unto death, even the death of the cross. Be that as it may, in the book of Revelation the picture of an eagle is applied to Jesus Christ when he vindicates his people from the dragon (12:14).

The purpose behind God's mighty victory is revealed in the words "brought you to myself." This is the point of redemption from Egypt. True, the people were Freed from bondage and oppression; true, they became an independent nation. In any case, the larger concept is that God was redeeming them for himself. He was their goal and destiny; they were to find their purpose and fulfillment in him, not in earthly freedom and independence.

A same truth underlies salvation in the New Testament. Jesus died and rose again not only to save us from the grip of sin, but also to bring us to God (I Pet. 3:18).

The Christian isn't set free to live it up or enjoy himself, but to give himself as a willing slave to the Lord (Rom. 12:1, 2).

The full significance of salvation by faith is that the people who receive Jesus Christ are not their own; they belong to him because he bought them with his blood (I Cor. 6:19, 20; II Cor. 5:15).

God's Promise
(v. 5)

Having reminded the people of what he had accomplished on their behalf, God now starts to divulge the terms on which he was going to bring the Israelites into a close and peculiar relation to himself. Their responsibility is unmistakable: "obey with my voice and keep my covenant."

Consequently, God would make them his very own possession among all the people of the earth.

He could do this because he owned the earth and in fact the whole universe.

Maybe coming out of the idolatry of Egypt the Israelites had not yet acknowledged the way that God was no mere national divinity. Nor would they be able to completely appreciate the depth of God's grace and mercy toward them, but they could find tremendous security in knowing that they belonged to an all-powerful God.

They were his special possession, chosen of all the people of the earth, not on the grounds that they had effectively merited it (deserved it), but basically because it pleased God to do it.

The words "my own possession" designate a costly possession acquired with exertion and carefully protected. This great truth-God's loving choice of these people - underlies both their privileges and their duties.

The same truth applies to Christians in the New Testament. Chosen in Christ, we are the recipients of his eternal love. Because God didn't spare his Son, believers enjoy the fullness of God's gifts (Rom. 8:28-39).

Simultaneously, our commitment to him means an life of obedient discipleship; Christians

are to obey Christ's voice and keep his commands
(John 14:21, 23).

The Status God Gives His People
(v. 6)

The Israelites were becoming a new political
entity, however at the start God advises them that
they are to be from all the other nations. They are
to be "a kingdom of priests and a holy nation."
This couldn't be said of some other people; the
tribes and nations of the world floundered in
pagansim, idolatry, and moral corruption.

In God's plan every person was to be holy.
Obviously, God later instituted the priesthood
for the performance of sacred duties regarding
tabernacle and temple worship, but this was not
to supplant the concept that each Israelite was
to walk in obedience to God and in personal
fellowship with him.

Ideally, every citizen was to unite in himself
the attributes of a king and a priest. The Israelites
were to be a royal and priestly race. Israel was not
to be a kingdom in the modern political sense,
but in the ancient Hebrew sense of the people

themselves were to be royalty to God. Such was their exalted position before him.

Their status as a holy nation was to isolate (separate) from surrounding corruption and defilement. Israel was set apart to preserve the knowledge and worship of the one true God. Israel's holiness consisted in its special consecration to the Lord. Israel was sacred by adoption. "Holy" here means unadulterated (pure), spotless (clean), clear from all pollution, bodily or spiritual.

In the New Testament, Peter uses this equivalent expression to describe the Christian's position (I Pet. 2:9 KJV).

The Response Of The People
(vv. 7-9)

Moses came back from his mountain meeting place with the Lord and reported back to the elders. These were the delegates of the whole nation. Authority was vested in the individuals who by explanation of age and experience were thought best qualified to rule. Israel had elders from the time of the captivity (Exod. 3:16 KJV). They were most likely the heads of families.

Moses needed to clarify the compact that God had proposed with Israel, since it required some response from the people. The elders thus disclosed it to the people. The multitudes promptly consented to comply with the Lord, and this was passed on to Moses, who gave the verdict to the Lord.

By their answer the people consented to accept God's covenant and the conditions of their special relationship to him. This was an essential condition for their total admission into the state of a royal priesthood. Their agreement was really a vow of allegiance and submission to God as their lawful ruler and sovereign. Having accepted the particulars of the contract, they can not change it in any way. The terms are lawfully official (legally binding).

Sinai was no way halting-point on the journey to Canaan, but the objective of the exodus journey in its first stage. God's people were redeemed by the blood of the lamb (12:13), given God's guidance (13:21, 22), and separated from the world (14:27-31).

Now they are about to come under God's detailed requirements for their daily life and worship (20:1-24:8). The covenant proposed by

God was not a means of salvation, however a pattern of life whereby his people were to show their sonship with God and their status as his redeemed people.

Having agreed to the covenant, the people are now to see the manifestation of God's presence and to hear his voice, that they might be deeply affected by his majesty, the awesomeness of the bond to be made, and truth of what Moses will impart to them as God's demands. To begin with, the Lord discloses to Moses that he will accredit him as his envoy (messenger) before the people (v. 9).

(When you come before the Lord in worship, what do you need to be reminded of? About God? About yourself? What things has God vowed to accomplish for you? What are you responsible for? In what manner should believers today show before a watching world their unmistakable connection to God? Were the Israelites rash and self-confident about their answer to God? Why or why not? How might one be realistic about himself and still make a commitment to obey the Lord?)

The Promised Land
(Deu. 11:8, 9)

The words of Moses to the people in Deuteronomy were spoken following forty years of wandering in the wilderness. He gave these messages around 1260 B. C. on the fields of Moab, on the eve of entry to the Promised Land. Deuteronomy is a repetition (restatement) and reaffirmation of the Sinai covenant.

The Laws recorded in Exodus, Leviticus, and Numbers are united and applied explicitly to the settled life in Canaan which is about to begin. In these verses we have a brief statement of the primary responsibility of the people.

Take Possession Of It
(v. 8)

Moses again expresses the duty and advantages of obedience to God. In chapters 10 and 11, in actuality, he says, "Remember God's love, his power, his provision, his law, his judgments. And let that memory keep you humble, faithful, and obedient."

In particular, in 11:1-7, he gives a short summary of the miracles and marvels of judgment that God had done in securing their release from Pharaoh, just as those he had done in the wilderness.

"Therefore" (v. 8) alludes back to these great events which form the basis of God's appeal for obedience. As the people obeyed God, they would find strength to possess Canaan. The Promised Land, obviously, was occupied by other tribes and Israel would have to battle for it. In any case, here God promised that he would give them power for the task.

Whatever commands God gives us, if we obey them, we will find inner spiritual power. For the present Christian, the indwelling Christ is strength for all his needs (Phil. 4:13). However to find Christ's strength, we should obey his commands.

Live Long In It
(v. 9)

Moses helped the people to remember God's promise to give them a land of their own. It would be a land filled with rich blessings; they could anticipate a prosperous future. God gave them each encouragement to move forward, but their enjoyment of his provisions would depend upon their obedience to him.

Their Special Responsibility
(Deu. 11:18, 19)

These verses are the practical key to progress for the Israelites in their new pursuit, just as for us today. There could be no triumph without remembering and teaching God's Word.

Remember God's Word
(v. 18)

"Lay up these words of mine in your heart and your soul" is the best approach to keep the human will in touch with God's will. It is with the will that God is to be looked for (4:29), loved (6:5), and served (10:12 NIV).

Since fiendish thoughts emerge in our minds and hearts, and because our corrupt nature proposes approaches to resist God and live freely of him, we should soak our minds with God's promise. The fight is for the mind, and God has given us the weapons to win.

Be that as it may, laying up his word requires a plan; it requires time and discipline. To do this we should read, study, meditate, memorize, and take an interest in Bible-teaching ministries of the church. God's word won't fill our hearts and minds if we fill them with newspapers, magazines, and TV.

Teach God's Word
(v. 19)

The picture here includes both precise Bible teaching of children and regular discussion about God and his word. God's word won't hop into the minds and hearts of our children by itself.

Nor would we be able to give the responsibility of teaching God's word to other people. Principally, the commitment rests with parents, who, obviously, can be helped by Sunday teachers, youth leaders, ministers, pastors and Christian day school teachers.

The purpose of consistent talking about God's word is to show how it relates to everyday life. Here is trust in God that applies to all that we do, not simply to church-going. Obeying and teaching his word is the way to build strong lives, families, and churches.

(What practical steps would you be able to share that have helped you obey vv. 8 and 9? For what reason do a few families fail in this significant issue? What help do you need from God to overcome some new land, as it were? Had you been an Israelite, do you believe you would have had strong faith to enter Canaan? Why or why not?)

Christians need daily to describe the privileges and responsibilities of belonging to God. They need also to teach these in their children. Christianity isn't attempting to keep numerous inconceivable standards; it is enjoying freedom and power to live as God wants one to live.

Chapter Seven

A Worshiping People
(Exod. 33:9-16; 35:29 NIV)

PEOPLE HAVE DIFFERENT CONCEPTS of worship. For a some, it might be synonymous with going to church. Others may consider wonderful organ music or the choir. You will find individuals who say they love the outdoors, viewing a splendid dusk maybe. Many Christians liken the sermon and prayers with worship.

Then again, in spite of the fact that it may not be religious worship, there are persons who worship their vehicles, their garments, their goods, their games, and their recreation. These things are nothing but idols, since they give their time, cash, strength, and loving affection to them.

It is hard to find a meaning of worship that suits all these mainstream ideas. In fact, worship is the thing that creatures give to the Creator. It involves the recognition of the superiority of deity. It implies that a person accepts his humanity and takes his responsibility to God seriously.

True worship has no meaning apart from man's accepting his place under the power of (Sovereignty of) God. Since God will be God, and on the grounds that man will be man, worship is necessary. It could well be said that God made man to worship him.

Consequently, the vital question of man's presence is whether he will worship God or something else. Anthropologists note that in every culture human beings are worshiping creatures.

Today we associate worship with the church, but the concept is far more extensive than the activities that happen on Sunday in a church building. Worship is on a very basic level merely one's attitude to the Almighty. Will I recognize him as God of my life, or will I select someone else or thing as more important than God?

When people go to the church building on Sunday to worship, they might be seeking ways to confess their obedience to God, or they may simply be experiencing (going through) a social everyday routine. One's attitude of heart in relation to God makes all the difference between true and false worship (fake worship).

How Moses And The People Worshiped (Exod. 33:9-11 NIV)

The picture here is of the most crude custom (primitive ritual). God's people had worshiped him previously, as during their joyous celebration of Pharaoh's thrashing and their triumph at the crossing of the Red Sea. In any case, no endorsed strategy for worship had been given to them.

Their ancestors had worshiped God in an assortment of ways and at different places. Here and there they built special altars at places where God had revealed himself to them. Be that as it may, more often than not their worship was basic (very simple); it was personal, family-focused, and didn't include elaborate ceremonies. Most importantly, Abraham's relatives were in the places of breaking away from customs of surrounding idol-worshipers.

The most significant truth about worship that the Israelites should pass on was that God is one, all inclusive, incomparable, supreme being who isn't to be represented by any manmade idol. Nor is he to be worshiped alongside other gods.

In any case, it wasn't long after the Israelites professed their eagerness and willingness to obey God that they fell into idol worship. While Moses was away on Mount Sinai receiving the laws from God, the people make a golden calf and worshiped it (Exod. 32).

God passed judgment on his people harshly, but Moses intervened for them and God promised again to take them to the Promised Land. Be that as it may, God warned, "I will not go up among you, lest I consume you in the way, for you are a stiff-necked people" (33:3 NIV).

Now we learned how Moses started a pattern of personal worship that soon affected the people. He was seeking direction and consolation from the Lord because of this disastrous turn of events.

Moses Set The Standard
(vv. 9, 10)

Up 'til now there was no tabernacle and no system of ritual worship and sacrifice. Moses basically set up a common portable shelter (a tent) far from the main camp and considered it the "tent of meeting" (v. 7). It might have been simply the tent that he usually lived in himself.

Its distance from the main camp served to represent the point that the individuals had relinquished (forfeited) God's presence by their idolatry. Moses, obviously, was the person who passed on God's messages to the people. He had met God on the mountain. Now he establishes a place where he could go to worship and commune with God.

As he did as such, two things occurred: The pillar of cloud, meaning God's presence, came to rest at the tent door, and the people likewise worshiped at their very own tents. In this way did Moses inspire the people to pursue his example. The people had been truly repentant after the failure of the golden calf (cf. 33:4-6). Their demeanor (attitude) of humility before God carried over in their worship.

There is no data here about the details of how the people worshiped God. However, the general spirit of their worship can be found from the context. The people had been dreadful in light of God's judgment and due to the terrible news that God would not go with them from there on.

Therefore, you can envision their joy when they once again recognized God's presence in the pillar of cloud. This was an encouraging sign to them. Also, it was encouraging to see how Moses kept on being their mediator, pleading their case before the Lord.

They recognized what Moses was doing when he went into the tent. They responded in worship because his intercession would mean forgiveness for them.

True worship occurs when people stand in the presence of God and praise him for his mercy and forgiveness. There can be no worship without this inner conviction that God is with us. Why go to church if you would prefer not to meet the living God? Why worship if you would prefer not to express gratitude (thanksgiving) toward God for his many mercies and blessings to you?

Here, in their simple way, the people could not confuse ritual and liturgy with the heart of worship. They felt overwhelmed (in awe of God) of God; no big wonder they rose up and worshiped. Worship can't be forced; it must emerge from within. It grows out of an awareness of who God is and what he has done for us.

Almost certainly the people were appreciative (thankful); they likewise were expectant and prayerful. They wanted to hear God's word through Moses and they wanted to seek God's protection and guidance. So today these two aspects of worship continue being imperative to God's people. They gather to hear the word of the

Lord and to supplicate, not as onlookers, however as respondents and participants.

We lose the imperativeness of worship if we think it is something proficient ministers or pastors are paid to do. They are worship leaders, but every Christian is a worshiper in his own right.

God Met With Moses
(v. 11)

Only Moses and Joshua really entered the special tent, however God acknowledged the worship of the others at their own tents. What occurred inside the tent of meeting? God and Moses had fellowship; the Lord spoke with Moses similarly as with a companion (friend).

The expression, "face to face," isn't to be taken physically (cf. vv. 17-23). It is used to demonstrate the intimacy of fellowship. True worship is portrayed as a meeting of good friends. That is the basic character of Christian worship. The special tent was classified "the tent of meeting" because that is the thing that occurred there; the Lord and Moses had a meeting.

It is possible for any Christian to meet God the same way now; that experience isn't limited to Moses and Joshua, or to pastors and ministers. Worship happens when God and his friends meet together, regardless of whether with regards to a church meeting, or in the family circle, or by yourself.

This simple portrayal of worship can enable any believer to understand what it is. How would you meet God up close and personal (face to face) today? The appropriate response is, By meditating in the Scriptures and praying. That is personal, private worship, but the same principles apply to corporate and family worship.

God's word must be central, in preaching just as well as reading. At that point, believers must have an opportunity to communicate (express themselves) to God. This they do by singing and praying.

Worship would transformed for any Christian, if he could envision meeting the living God vis-à-vis (face to face). The people who lead in worship and the people who preach should to consistently lead the worshiper to this experience.

(What is worship? What makes worship significant for a Christian? How would you assess worship at your church? What means the presence of the Lord in your worship? For what reason is it critical to meet God in worship every day? In what way would Christians be able to cultivate the kind of relationship Moses had with the Lord?)

Moses Sought God's Presence
(Exod. 33:12-16 KJV)

Moses had been commanded by the Lord to lead Israel to the Promised Land (33:1-3). Having recently seen Israel's idolatry, Moses realized what a troublesome and difficult undertaking this would be, aside from God's ever-present guidance and protection. In these verses we learn how Moses brought this deeply close to home problem to the Lord and how God answered him.

The Request Of Moses
(vv. 12, 13)

The preceding verses portrayed how Moses worshiped God, but the view is from outside. Now we are permitted inside the tent of meeting to hear what went on between Moses and God.

Supplication is an essential part of worship. Fellowship with God in worship means conversing with him and hearing his voice. This is the thing that occurred on this event.

Moses had a request to make to the Lord. He reminded God of his command to lead the people to the Promised Land, but since God himself had said that he was not going with them (v. 3). Moses needed to know whom God would send. God had said a angel would go with Moses and the Israelites (v. 2). Obviously Moses needed to know who this angel would be.

This request is based on the special relationship Moses enjoyed with God. Since Moses had found favor in God's sight, he could approach the Lord about this issue. Moses had cultivated his own insight into God through worship.

God had singled out Moses (3:4 KJV) to be the recipient of a special revelation and to be the deliverer of Israel, however Moses needed to grow in his comprehension of God's presence and his purpose.

If a person responds to God's call to salvation in Christ, he begins to know God in a different way. God becomes personal; worship is the growth of a personal relationship. Accordingly, when basic needs arise for God's guidance, the worshiper doesn't hesitate to express himself to God in terms of God's promises.

The Christian has found favor with God, through the death and resurrection of Jesus Christ. Along these lines, in his worship experiences he can approach God certainly about anything by any stretch of the imagination.

As indicated by v. 13, Moses needed reassurance. Worship includes asking God for that, as well. "Show me now thy ways" implies that Moses was requesting a preview of how God was going to be faithful to his promises. Moses needed some unmistakable tangible proof of God's special calling. If indeed he had been singled out for this responsibility, it would be essential for him to make certain of God's presence before he began to move.

Moses reminded God of his interesting relationship with the nation in general; the Israelites were his people. This implied the duty regarding their consideration at last was God's, not Moses'.

In our worship experiences we not only express gratitude toward God for past blessings, but in addition for his promise for what's to come. Every open door for personal and corporate worship should find the believer gaining new expectation (hope) and assurance for what lies ahead. We have to remind ourselves and the Lord to remember his promises, and after that request that he do them while we are in the amidst life's battles.

Christians are his people. It is God's presence, in worship as well as consistently, that gives us assurance and marks us out as his people. Moses didn't need the land that is known for promise without God; it is his presence that makes every experience profitable and encouraging.

God's Promise Of His Presence
(v. 14)

This is God's answer to Moses' petition. God will go with Moses and the people. Further, the troublesome adventure (difficult journey) would arrive at a victorious conclusion: "I will give you rest." This was the typical statement for the possession of the Promised Land (cf. Deu. 3:20; Josh. 1:13 NIV).

This is a noteworthy promise, taking into account how the people had recently failed the Lord. Moses had persisted in looking for the Lord in spite of the obvious defeat. His worship was seriously functional, intensely practical. For him, the knowledge of God meant an intimate walk with God in each experience.

Moses was not a conqueror searching for new lands; he wanted unmistakably far more than physical triumph; he wanted God's presence for himself and the people.

When Christians are faithful in giving God their obedience and their praise, they will get all the assurance they need of his presence. Jesus promised God's presence for the people who love and obey him (John 14:21, 23 NIV).

It is the point at which we misbehave (step out of line) with God's will that we lose the feeling of his presence. Obviously, God doesn't leave us, but our awareness of his presence (the sense of his presence) is darkened when we disobey him.

By worshiping God we can give new insight into his living will and plans for us. We are not given a preview of how he will function in our lives; we don't have the foggiest idea what the following day will bring. Be that as it may, his presence is a higher priority than all else.

As the author of Hebrews clarifies: "For he (God) has said, 'I will never fail you nor forsake you.' Hence we can unquestionably say, "The Lord is my helper, I will not be afraid; what can man do to me? (13:5, 6 NIV)

This helps us to understand why neglecting personal, family, and public worship is so grievous, so disastrous. We simply lose our orientation (our bearings) and our knowledge of God's presence. The Christian who is not faithful in worship is a disabled Christian (a crippled Christian).

Moses got the answer because he knew what it meant to converse with God. Moses was not afraid to confess his need to the Lord, and God gave him the reassurance he needed.

God's Presence Made His People Distinctive (vv. 15, 16)

Moses disclosed (told) God he would not go without his presence. Unless God went with him and the Israelites, they would just resemble the various wicked nations around them. This is the thing that gave them their particular distinctive character. Moses saw the central issue unmistakably. Better to stay in the wilderness than go to Canaan without the Lord.

The people of God today should be known by the manner in which they mirror God's presence to other people. When unbelievers come to church, what impressions do they get about God from the manner in which Christians worship? Israel was a marked nation for God's glory. Christians, as well, must be the interpretation of the particular distinctive character of God's presence.

(How does worship help to set you up to meet life? In what circumstances do you feel an uncommon need for God's presence? How would you think public, private, and family worship can be better identified with life's needs? "In thy going with us...we are distinct," Moses told God. How might this be proven in your church? Your family? Your own life?)

The People Gave Willingly
(Exod. 35:29)

While on Mount Sinai Moses had received guidelines for development (construction) of the tabernacle (Exod. 25-27). Now the time had come to construct this place of worship. Consequently, God commanded that an offering be taken (35:5).

This chapter depicts the astonishing response of God's people. Verse 29 is a summary of the event. It demonstrates various intriguing certainties that apply to Christian worship today.

Their giving emerged out of their souls. They were moved by a longing to obey the Lord. Moses had the plans, but the people needed to give wholeheartedly before anything could be possible.

Their offering was a freewill offering to the Lord. It was not some sort of church charge. Whatever was given, from adornments to material, was given to God for his purposes. Obviously, it was expensive, but that made the experience of giving significantly increasingly important.

A significant part of worship is liberal, willing giving of our means. Time after time people come to church just to get something, not to give something. Obviously, God gives us something when we meet him - encouragement, expectation (hope), guidance, love, etc. Be that as it may, the Lord's blessing is advanced by conciliatory giving.

Conclusion: Often the embodiment of Christian worship is lost in the gear that goes with it. We stress the choir, the furnishings, the preacher's style; we stress over how we and other people look.

Thus, we miss the Lord himself. At that point we inquire as to why the distinctive Christian power is absent. If we don't find Christ in our worship, we have lost the purpose of it.

Chapter Eight

The Fulfillment Of The Promise Delayed
` (Unbelief Delays Covenant Fulfillment)
(Num. 13:30-14:10a NIV)

The Lord Jesus Christ showed that unbelief is the sin that condemns people. "He who doesn't believe is condemned already, because he had not believed in the name of the only Son of God," he said (John 3:18 NIV).

The central issue of the Bible is whether people believe God. Every experience can be diminished to that question. One's response to this question influences life now and in the Age to come.

Beginning with Adam and Eve, people have had to choose whether or not God is to be believed and obeyed. The Bible doesn't separate belief and obedience. Actually, the Bible speaks much about the risk of deception, false belief of outward profession without inner change, of promising to believe but not following through with obedience.

That is the reason Jesus cautioned, "Not every one who says to me, "Lord, Lord," shall enter the kingdom of heaven, but he who does the will of my Father who is in heaven" (Matt. 7:21 NIV).

Today in every public survey that is taken, most by far of people who profess to believe in God. But there is no doubt that with regards to their obedience to the will of God, there is little proof of a changed behavior.

Jesus made it clear on numerous occasions that true profession of faith in God will prompt (lead to) a personal commitment to the Son of God as Lord and Savior. When he was asked, "What must we do, to be doing the works of God?" Jesus answered, "This is the work of God, that you have believe in him whom he has sent" (John 6:28 29 NIV).

In the present lesson we experience a horrendous, frightful experience. The Israelites, who professed faith in God, didn't obey his will when the open door came to hold onto the Promised Land. Today God also tests the commitment of those who claim to be his. Open doors for obedience are surrounding us; over and over again even Christians are paralyzed by unbelief.

The Evil Report
(Num. 13:30-33 KJV)

The Israelites camped at Sinai for a year while God taught them in his laws and gave them plans for the construction of the tabernacle. The book of Numbers begins with the nation's census - taking: About three weeks after the fact the people began the march to Canaan, moving from Sinai to Kadesh in eleven days (Deu. 1:2 KJV).

Numbers 13 begin with the mission of twelve men, one from every tribe, who were supposed "to spy out the land." Moses gave them explicit things to search for and requested that they bring back some fruit of the land, which they did.

At that point, after forty days, the people gathered to hear the report and see the fruit. The covert agents (spies) liked the gainful capability (potential) of the land, but they didn't care for the strength of the people who were living there (vv. 27-29).

Caleb's Call For Action
(v. 30)

Apparently the individuals reacted with anxious fear as a result of what they had been told, in light of the fact that Caleb, one of the twelve covert agents (spies), needed to calm them before he could make a proposal.

Caleb detected what the state of mind of the people was turning negative, so he hopped in without a moment's delay with his inspirational (encouragement) statements and activity. He encouraged quick control of Canaan since he persuaded the Israelites could overcome the opposition.

Amidst this dismal story of unbelief and defiance (rebellion), Caleb - later joined by Joshua - stands apart as a man of faith. Caleb didn't dispute the realities of the report, however he appropriately detected that if victory somehow were to be won, the people needed to move right away. He knew that the more they contemplated the tenants of Canaan, the harder it is attack (to take the offensive).

This is a basic principle of the Christian life. Delayed obedience is equivalent to disobedience, and more often than not it usually brings disaster. It often is hard to regain one's spiritual imperativeness (vitality), if obedience to what God says isn't prompt.

It is imperative to note now in the story that the verifiability of the covert (spy) operatives' report isn't being questioned. Three highlights of the report are critical in the light of present day archaeological discoveries. To start with, the reference to milk and honey was a traditional description of a productive, fruitful land; it was used as early as as 2000 b.C. of the area north of Galilee.

Second, the reference to fortified cities has been confirmed. Various walled cities, five to fifteen or twenty acres of land in size, were scattered over the land. Third, the population was a mixed one. Ancient records show the presence of Amorites, Hittites, Canaanites, and Indo-Europeans.

The Amorites came to Palestine before 2000 B.C. furthermore, are known to have lived in the mountains east and west of Jordan. The Hittites were off-shoots of the great Hittite empire in Asia Minor. The Canaanites inhabited the fertile regions of the Jordan valley and the coastlands. The Amalekites were nomads. (The events between the Exodus and the occupation of Canaan by Israel happened somewhere in the range of 1300 and 1200 B.C.

The Majority's Call For Inaction
(vv. 31-33)

Now the other covert operatives (spies) began to decipher the realities. Prior to Caleb's call for quick activity, they had just announced what they had found. Now they contest Caleb's interpretation and produce what is designated "a evil report."

To begin with, they concluded that it was inconceivable for Israel to possess the Promised Land in light of the fact that the people there were more grounded (stronger) than the Israelites (v. 31). Indeed, they were strong and they did live in invigorated urban communities (fortified cities), but would they say they were stronger than Israel?

That was an instance of personal judgment, not of fact. So the body of evidence begins to mount against obedience and favor disobedience. Unbelief is picking up that advantage or gaining the upper hand. We should always be cautious how we decipher what we see, with the goal that we don't make either untimely or mistaken judgments or decisions.

Satan always attempts to get God's people to misread the facts, so the they appear to have adequate avocation for not doing what God wants.

For this situation, the covert agents (spies) intensified the circumstance and made it difficult for the people to obey God since they began to embellish the facts with misrepresentations. They expressed two words:

(1) The Land devours it inhabitants. This could mean various things. It could imply that they thought Canaan was presented to unending assaults from surrounding tribes, with the goal that its tenants consistently must be armed and watchful.

Or on the other hand, it could imply that throughout their ventures (travels) to every part of the covert operatives (spies) saw a considerable number of funeral services, immense quantities of the Canaanites being cut off at that time. In any case, it would not incline one to move there.

Every one of the people were "men of great stature," enormous men, maybe giants. Here is the where lying bamboozled them in their endeavors to induce the people not to go. True, the "sons of Anak" were rumored to be a race of Goliaths, but unquestionably not "every one of the people were giants.

This part of their appeal was obviously false. Be that as it may, these covert agents (spies) needed to emphasize the worst about the circumstance, so they singled out the few great warriors they had seen.

Subsequently, the men of Israel thought about themselves as grasshoppers as opposed to the giants, and the covert operatives (spies) included this was the manner in which the goliaths saw them, as well. How could they find this out? This was basically some portion of their tricky system (their treacherous strategy) to undermine Caleb's call for action. You can well envision how this people everywhere were beginning to feel about moving into Canaan.

By interpreting the facts in the most exceedingly terrible conceivable light, the covert agents (spies) produced fear and this led to disobedience, stagnation, and defeat.

Caleb stated, "We are well able..." but the others said, "We are not...." What had the difference in their conclusions? How would we some of the time attempt to "stack the deck" against obeying the Lord? What defenses have you used? In what capacity would Christians be able to take a look at life's challenges but have a positive attitude?

What opportunities face your church, your family, your own life that may bring about clashing or conflicting opinions? How might you beat fear of taking risks and meeting possible defeat?

The People's Despair
(Num. 14:1-5)

Roosted on the doorsteps of the Promised Land, the people of Israel by the by floundered despondently (wallowed in despair). These verses uncover the inauspicious actualities of the case. It is hard to accept that these were same ones who had so sublimely celebrated triumph over Pharaoh two brief years prior. However our own memories of God's victories are famously short when we meet a new trial and test of our faith.

They Wept
(v. 1)

This was a bleak, dismal night in the camp of Israel. The discouraging interpretation of the land won the day. Subsequently, the people went through the night in grieving, on the grounds that they had chosen their case was miserable. They accepted the most exceedingly awful, and in the event that the most noticeably awful would work out as expected, at that point they ought to in reality cry.

This is a delineation of how an enormous gathering can be influenced by the assessments of a few. The people knew God's promises, they knew his power by experience, but their knowledge was not adequate to shield them from accepting the evil report.

Obviously, this also demonstrates the basic job of the chosen few. The people were at their benevolence (mercy). How often God's will is missed in light of the fact that a couple of willingly volunteers choose. With obligation regarding framing assessments comes magnificent responsibility before God, if God's people are driven adrift (led astray).

They Complained To Moses
About Their Fate
(vv. 2-4)

The Israelites looked for a substitute for their situation and they found Moses and Aaron, their

God-designated leaders. "Murmur" signifies to grumble and criticize. Now we see the strange ends their pessimism led them to.

They saw the opposition in Canaan so imposing that they decided it would have been better to die in Egypt or in the wilderness, than to attempt to occupy Canaan. They essentially decided that there was no possibility to succeed.

If they moved forward, their wives and children would be wiped out. In this way, it is smarter to come back to Egypt.

Obviously, they had no way of knowing the future, regardless of whether they went on to Canaan or returned to Egypt. Their disobedience delivered such misery that they couldn't think either logically or spiritually.

Their minds were obscured, their hearts overwhelmed - all because they wouldn't accept God's good and perfect will. This is the cost of disobedience each Christian ought to gauge (weigh).

What is most noticeably terrible, they accused everything on God (v. 3). They couldn't see that the God who had delivered them from Egypt could likewise vanquish their enemies in Canaan. They not only gave up hope, they also blamed

God for bringing them to the point of obliteration (destruction).

Christians today frequently neglect to see that obstacles and trials are a test of their obedience and faith. They conclude that God is out to make them as hopeless and miserable as could be expected under the circumstances. They choose ahead of time that things are going to turn out in the worst or most awful possible way. Each obstacle is really a chance to obey God despite what the outward appearance appear to be.

Assuming, in any case, we abandon God, we can't in any way, shape or form take a look at facts sensibly or realistically. People of faith don't pretend the adversary isn't there; they know the issues of life are real, but they persist in obedience to what they know is God's will, committing the consequences to him.

The rebellion of the Israelites was profound to such an extent that they considered choosing another leader to return them to Egypt. (Nehemiah says they actually did so; cf. 9:17 KJV). The discourteousness and lack of gratitude of the people merited God's later judgment: that generation was banished from entering the Promised Land.

Dr. John Thomas Wylie

They were punished by their wishes being granted to die in the wilderness. Sadly, their conduct too often is paralleled by certain Christians today, who shrink from the smallest difficulty and remain captives, slaves to sin rather than attempt to move to a higher level of spiritual reality.

Moses And Aaron Prostrated Themselves (v. 5)

The astonishing unbelief and rebellion of the people drove Moses and Aaron to fall on the ground before them. They begged the people to believe and obey the Lord. Moses said, "Don't be in dread or afraid of them (the occupants of Canaan).

The Lord your God who goes before you will himself fight for you, just as he did for you in Egypt before your eyes" (Deu. 1:29 NIV).

Clearly, after they failed to discourage the people, Moses and Aaron also appealed to the Lord. Most likely they asked him to soften the hearts of the rebellious, to give them mental fortitude (courage) and faith to move ahead. At this crucial point in time God himself was the only refuge Moses and Aaron had from the turbulent, stiff-necked rabble.

God answered their supplication (vv. 10b-12), but the response (answer) was judgment for sin. God had wrought more than enough signs (that anyone could believe) for them to believe in him, his love, and his power, but they didn't believe; rather, they despised the Lord.

(Ask somebody to ponder the purposes behind what valid reason they now and again have fallen into despair. Request that somebody share personally. What influenced their judgment at times in this way? For what reason does the clouded side so frequently prevail in our reasoning?

How might we strengthen our minds and hearts with the truth with regards to God, so we won't fall hostage to hopelessness and destruction? What affliction do you face since you discover hard to surmount with fortitude and expectation? What obstacles in your mind have kept you from obeying God?)

The Faith Of Joshua And Caleb
(Num. 14:6-10a NIV)

These two men of faith stand apart as brilliant lights against this dull scene. They would not buckle to the weight of defeat, disobedience and rebellion. Rather, they took the offensive for the Lord.

God Would Give Them The Land
(vv. 6-8 NIV)

In the first place, Joshua and Caleb "rent their clothes," which was an indication of humiliation and confession before the Lord for the sins of other people. This sin was not theirs, but they partook in its repercussions; they willingly volunteered, to be identified to such horrible disobedience.

At that point they spoke hopefully to the individuals, attempting to reverse the tide of pessimism. They helped them to remember both the goodness of Canaan itself and of God's promise to give it to them.

God would bring them into it because he delighted in them. Obviously, now Joshua and

Caleb surely understood that God's pleasure in Israel was dependent on Israel's obedience.

Joshua and Caleb tried to center the issue at the right place; the nation's special relation to God. The people knew the land was appealing; they had seen a portion of its produce (v. 23). But now they couldn't expedite themselves to press on. Their feeling of commitment to God ought to have inspired them even without the rich blessing of the land.

They Should Trust God And Not Rebel (v. 9)

Fear is a natural response, however in the event that we are deadened (paralyzed) by dread, then it has thwarted or hindered as opposed to helped us. Obviously, Israel feared the fight ahead, but that fear should not have brought rebellion against God. This is the thing that Caleb and Joshua opposed and spoke against. Twice they called for mental fortitude (courage) instead of fear. Rebellion was wrong, despite the fact that the enemies were great.

Attempting to manage fear, Caleb and Joshua spoke of how simple the triumph would be, on the grounds that God was with them. Is it safe to say that he was not sufficiently able to fight for them? Had he not crushed Pharaoh's military? God's power was with the end goal that the adversaries in Canaan would be "bread" for Israel, or, as we may state today, "a piece of cake."

For what reason would Israel vanquish Canaan? Since the armed forces there had lost their "protection." This word is taken from an Eastern articulation that implies cover from the scorching sun.

There would be no defense for them before the Israelites.

God had chosen to pass judgment on the inhabitants of Canaan at this time in light of the fact that their iniquity was completed (Gen. 15:16 KJV). This was part of his promise to Abraham.

We don't have the foggiest idea about God's eternal decrees and we don't have the foggiest idea about his timetable for the working out of them. Subsequently, we can't prejudge the result of any circumstance. When God calls us to obey him, we should do so and trust him to prepare the way for us.

The People Tried To Kill Them
(v. 10a)

So determined were the people to fall back that they attempted to stone the people who encouraged them to push ahead (move forward). The intrigue of Joshua and Caleb failed to attract anyone's attention (fell on deaf ears) and the hard hearts. Fortunately, they got away (escaped) and survived to lead the next generation into the Promised Land.

(How does God address Christians today, to enable them to change course and settle on the right decisions? What should an person do, if having disobeyed the Lord, he sees the mistakes of his ways?)

This is certainly not a wonderful story. It should instruct us that it's anything but a frivolous thing to disobey God's will. It ought to likewise demonstrate to us that it is so natural to be deceived or victimized by fear of conditions.

Jesus Christ never said that the life of discipleship would be easy. Faith is tried and tested. Difficulties come our way. Be that as it may, if we ask God for faith and mental fortitude (courage), he meets us at the purposes of our needs and our desires. Caleb and Joshua are examples of that.

Dr. John Thomas Wylie

Chapter Nine

Claiming The Promised Land
(Joshua 4:4-7; 5:10-12; 6:1-3; 11:23 KJV)

THE "IT ISN'T POSSIBLE" or the "it can't be done" attitude must be supplanted by "it very well may be done" or "it can be done" thinking if issues are to be comprehended and progressions made. This has been the sign of the advancement of the Western civilization progress. The endowments we have, all things considered, come to us because men of vision would have not surrendered to defeatist thinking.

Regardless of whether in science, medicine, industry, or warfare, the men who have led us have not been prevented by appearing inconceivabilities.

The church of Jesus Christ likewise has been blessed by men who have set out to challenge the negatives of others in the church who have liked to live with business as usual.

Today Christians are serving Jesus Christ from multiple points of view and places since they have tested fortifications of unbelief and the complacencies of unconcerned church people.

For these "we can do it" Christians, Joshua of old is the prototype. He embodies the spirit of fortitude and faith that moves mountains. In the present lesson we see how he vanquished the land that a generation of his companions thought was difficult to take.

The Memorial Of Crossing The Jordan (Josh. 4:4-7 KJV)

Joshua is a book of energizing triumphs for the Lord. It remains in striking differentiation to the grim record of Israel's unbelief and sin recorded in the book of Numbers. God's plan for Israel's immediate occupation of Canaan had been rejected when the people listened to the fearful, "evil" report of the scouting party (spies).

In judgment God said that none of the men who had seen his glory in Egypt and in the wilderness, but disobeyed his command to vanquish (conquer) Canaan, would ever live to see the Promised Land (cf. Num. 14:20-35).

Thus, "the people of Israel walked forty years in the wilderness, till all the nation, the men of war that came forth out of Egypt, perishd, on the grounds that they didn't hearken to the voice of the Lord" (Josh. 5:6 KJV).

Indeed, even Moses himself was not allowed to enter Canaan, since he and Aaron had sinned in striking the rock to get water (Num. 20:10-12; Deu. 3:2428 KJV), However, before Moses died, the Lord commissioned Joshua to lead the Israelites into Canaan (Deu. 31:23 KJV).

The book of Joshua takes the story of Israel's history on from the death of Moses, through the conquest of Canaan, to the death of Joshua. Chapter 1-12 cover the initial five or six years after Moses' death. Chapters 13-21 portray the distribution of the land among the twelve tribes. The events of the last two chapters presumably occurred around twenty years after the fact. The victory likely started around 1240 B. C.

Joshua was born in Egypt. He became Moses' right-hand man during the Exodus and desert wanderings. He was a fine military leader (Exod. 17:8ff NIV.).

He was Moses' companion in the law-giving at Sinai (Exod. 24:13). At Kedesh he was sent as one of the agents (spies) into Canaan, and with Caleb urged immediate occupation (Num.

14:6ff.). Therefore, these two men were the only ones to survive the wilderness wanderings.

Joshua was "full of the spirit of wisdom" (Deu. 34:9 ASV), yes he needed special encouragement from the Lord for his awesome obligations. He needed strength and fearlessness (courage); the key to his success was his obedience to the Lord and the Lord's presence with him (Josh. 1:1-9 ASV).

God promised to give him the land; God promised he would not fail him or forsake him. Joshua believed the promises and moved out to claim the land.

Twelve Stones From The River
(vv. 4-6)

The first obstruction that disrupted the general flow of Israel's success of Canaan was the Jordan River, which forms the eastern boundary of the nation. At the point when the individuals landed there, they found a further difficulty; the waterway was flooding (3:15). It was spring and the waterway was swollen with softened snows.

Be that as it may, God guided Joshua to a challenging step of faith. The priests were to lead the procession into the water, and when they ventured into it, the river would stop flowing. The priests obeyed this alarming and frightening command and the waters of the Jordan were cut off by a blockage sixteen miles upstream at Adam.

The priests stood in the middle of the dry river bed until the whole nation crossed into Canaan. (This is a same stretch of the Jordan where John the Baptist's ministry and Jesus's baptism occurred).

Once again God demonstrated and proved true to his promise. His power that the previous generation would not trust was put in plain view once again, and the people conquered what had all the earmarks of being an inconceivable deterrent. In any case, the priests had to venture out on that first step of faith into the water. They trusted God and obeyed him; that is the sure way to spiritual progress and victory.

This event was amazing to such an extent that God told Joshua to raise a special memorial. Twelve men were chosen to go to the river bed where the priests had stood. They represented the twelve tribes of Israel. Every one took a stone from the river and carried it toward the western shore.

A Reminder Of The Miracle
(v. 7)

The memorial stones were erected to impress succeeding generations with the power of God. "The waters of the Jordan were cut off" not by human creativity, but by God himself. You can well envision future generations asking how it was that Israel could cross the river.

The Israelites could assume nor claim no credit for it; the glory should go to God alone. Here was another confirmation (proof) of God's love and care for his people.

So in Israel's history this miracle ranks alongside the crossing of the Red Sea as a huge defining moment (or a turning point). The parting of the Red Sea secured escape from Egypt; the drying up of the Jordan secured passage into Canaan. Both could be accomplished only by a sovereign, loving God.

Christian families today need to set aside some time to help their children remember God's great intercession in history and in their own lives. In a time when supernatural occurrences (miracles) are questioned, and when the Old Testament stories are consigned to folklore or mythology.

Dr. John Thomas Wylie

Christians ought to affirm their faith in God's power to stop rivers, if necessary to accommodate his people. These supernatural occurrences (miracles) are recorded to strengthen our own certainty (confidence) in God. They are a witness to the world "that the hand of the LORD is mighty" (4:24 KJV).

The Fruit Of The Land
(Josh. 5:10-12 KJV)

The immediate consequence of the miraculous crossing of the Jordan was the melting away of the opposition in Canaan (5:1). The powers that the covert operatives (spies) had dreaded essentially broken (dissolved) down before God's power. Hence, the Israelites could unite their foothold in Canaan with safety.

The people who had been born in the wilderness had not been circumcised. Hence, there is a respite in Israel's advance so this ritual could be performed (5:2-9). It marked the renewal of the special relationship among God and his people. Genesis 17 describes the presentation of this practice, which later was incorporated into the Mosaic system regarding the Passover (Exod. 12:44 KJV).

The First Passover In Canaan
(v. 10)

Since the people were once again under an uncommon covenant with the Lord, the way was obvious to keep the Passover. Having been circumcised, every one of the men of Israel were equipped for the consecrated dining experience remembrance of God's redemption (deliverance) of them from Egypt.

These two grave functions - circumcision and the Passover - demonstrated undeniably that God had reestablished his people to himself and had put behind him the disobedience of the past generation.

The grace of God was again poured out on an undeserving people. His purposes were not frustrated by unbelief. He demonstrated again that he was fulfilling his original promises.

Fundamentally, both of these ceremonies were done on enemy territory. They were a preview of the victory to come. Israel had not yet needed to fight. God shielded them from encompassing tribes while they observed these special reminders of his unique relationship with them.

This was a time for renewed commitment (dedication) for who was to come. Worship came before battle. We do well to observe the same priority, despite the fact that now and again it may appear to be increasingly judicious to battle. Keep in mind the Lord first is God's order of conquest.

The First Produce Of The Land
(v. 11)

Here was another token of God's goodness; the Israelites could eat from the land itself, despite the fact that they had not worked for it. Evidently this was nourishment abandoned by the escaping tribes-people. The "parched grain" was the new harvest left lying in the fields.

The Last Manna
(v. 12)

Canaan had been promised as an inheritance to Israel, so the nourishment (food) was a preview of the full inheritance to come. Now there is no longer the need for divine provision of manna (cf. Exod. 16:35). In any case, it is significant that God had never backpedaled on his promise to provide food, even during those very long years in the wilderness.

The Victory At Jericho
(Josh. 6:1-3 RSV)

Now the Israelites face their first opposition in Canaan. They were camped at Gilgal, only a couple of miles from the stronghold city of Jericho, which had just been scouted (ch. 2). This time the operatives (spies) revealed that the inhabitants "are fainthearted because of us" (2:24 RSV). Yet the Lord graciously sent Joshua an extraordinary flag-bearer of consolation (a message of encouragement) before he started the assault on Jericho (5:13-15 RSV).

The story of the conquest which pursues demonstrates the divine authority directing Joshua's methodology. There were three phases in the triumph: (1) the capture of Jericho and Ai, chapters 6-8, which opened up the passes into the interior of the nation.

A wedge was along these lines driven between the northern and southern areas of the nation. (2) The destruction of the southern alliance, chapters 9, 10; (3) the defeat of the northern alliance, chapter 11.

The City Under Siege
(v. 1)

This verse is an incidental clarification of conditions in Jericho, coming only preceding the directions for Joshua from the commander of the Lord's army. This is a realistic depiction of how Israel's presence influenced the nearby people.

They had retreated within the city walls and remained there. Jericho, an antiquated post city critical, was situated on the fields of Jordan around seventeen miles east of Jerusalem. The mountains of Judea rise unexpectedly from the fields just toward the west of Jericho.

God's Promise Of Victory
(v. 2)

This is a level promise from the Lord to Joshua, who by this time had probably been contemplating how to assault the city. Jericho is imagined as a piece of fruit ready for Joshua's picking; it is as of now comparable to in his grasp. Despite the fact that it was secured by "mighty men of valor," God would defeat their opposition and empower Israel to triumph.

Once more, God gives his leader the important consolation. It is hard for us to acknowledge what this more likely than not intended to Joshua. He had brought the people crosswise over Jordan, on account of a powerful supernatural occurrence (miracle), but how was God going to give now? "I will be with you," God had promised, and here is the fulfillment of his promise.

God's people often are gone up against by halting spots where they need to hold tight for guidelines from God. At such occasions they should concentrate on God himself, instead of on the size and power of the deterrent. In due time God will reveal a promise to claim, maybe a word from Scripture, or the consolation of a companion.

God's Plan Of Battle
(v. 3)

This was an strange plan undoubtedly. As opposed to assault legitimately, the Israelites were to walk around Jericho six days, once each day. On the seventh day they were to walk around Jericho seven times, with trumpets blowing. At a special signal, the Israelites were to shout and the city's walls would fall.

No commander had ever assaulted a walled city along these lines. The standard technique was to lay a foundation against the wall and attempt to get a few men over it. This was an expensive strategy. However there was something to be said for God's strategy.

This was extremely a war of nerves against the men of Jericho; for quite a while they would see the encompassing soldiers and wonder what the Israelites were doing.

Be that as it may, there was a spiritual factor moreover. The priests were included. The ark of the covenant was carried by them, symbolizing God's presence. There was likewise the imagery of the number seven: seven priests, seven trumpets, seven days, seven circuits of the city on the seventh day.

The majority of this showed the flawlessness, culmination, and fulfillment of God's plan.

The entire thing was expected to impress the Canaanites with a feeling of divine power, just as to move the Israelites to faith and trust in the Lord. Unquestionably Joshua and his people needed to trust in God for the execution of this abnormal plan, on the grounds that all by itself there was no chance they could catch the city just by walking around it.

God again demonstrated consistent with his promise. Joshua obeyed the Lord's instructions precisely, and the city fell before the Israelites. This huge triumph was accomplished, against overwhelming opposition, because God's people believed he would act in response to their faith and obedience. That is the way in which spiritual headway is made in the Christian life.

The Conquest Completed
(Josh. 11:23 NIV)

This is the synopsis articulation toward the finish of the northern campaign. It uncovers the complete obedience of Joshua to the Lord's commands, and furthermore the faithfulness of God to the promises to Moses. Joshua "took" the land that the Lord had given Israel. By his

Dr. John Thomas Wylie

faithfulness to God he was empowered and enable to get what was offered in God's loving plan and provided by God's power.

The key to Joshua's conquest is found in the original instructions given to him by God. God revealed to him that that if he was mindful so as to do all that he instructed, he would "have great success." The blessing of God was related straightforwardly to Joshua's meditation in the law of God and his obedience to it (cf. 1:7, 8 NIV).

The present lessons and those earlier give a striking contrast between the results of obedience and disobedience to God. For disobedience the nation suffered forty long years and a whole generation lost its inheritance; for obedience the nation received victory and the fulfillment of God's promises.

Certainly there was a hard struggle, but by God's power and presence the Israelites prevailed "and the land had rest from war." God was faithful to his covenant; Christians may find him faithful to his word today. So Joshua is an encouragement for believers to persist in faith and obedience.

We have the opportunity to meditate in God's word day and night, and we can claim the presence of God in every situation. Regardless he still says: "Be not frightened, nor be dismayed; for the Lord your God is with you wherever you go" (1:9 NIV).

(How can we teach our children the great achievements of our faith and encourage them to trust in an all-powerful God? How would you have felt, had you been one of the priests at the edge of the flooding Jordan? For what reason would you have stepped in? For what reason would you have hesitated? What difficulties do you face in the way of your spiritual advancement?

In what power would Christians be able to find God's plan to defeated them? What insight does the New Testament have that would contrast with God's battle plan for spiritual warfare? What command and encouragement did God give Joshua that you find relevant to your needs? In what areas of spiritual leadership would you say you are seeking help?)

Conclusion: Analogies for Christian teaching can be drawn from the intrusion of Canaan. Spiritual issues of faith and obedience were in question at every step of the way. God gave Israel rest, which the unbelieving generation had failed to acquire (cf. Ps. 95:10, 11 NIV).

The New Testament shows this represents a spiritual principle substantial, valid for every generation (Heb. 4:1-11 KJV). The promise of God's "rest" is at last and completely fulfilled in Jesus Christ.

Chapter Ten

Difficulty In Keeping The Covenant
(Judg. 2:13-23)

UNFAITHFULNESS STANDS OUT AS truly newsworthy every single day, in the divorce procedures we see, in the general news (web, TV, PDAs) too. Actually, much is made of it, except if it in includes prominent people.

Quite a long while back when a leading Congressman was engaged with a dance club entertainer, his issue was splashed everywhere throughout the newspapers and television broadcasts.

In any case, unfaithfulness portrays other relationships also. Work and the executives blame each other for being unfaithful to campaign promises. Today, Whole nations are blamed for being unfaithful to settlements and treaties.

Therefore, society is filled with conflict because people think that its difficult and find it hard to keep their promises. Promises are broken without any potential repercussions, even by local officials. The explanation is that people put their very own advantages in front of their duties, and in the event that a promise is going to mean hardship, at that point the easy route is to dodge your commitments and accuse the other person.

Christians face the same pressures. They are not immune to the temptations to renege on commitments. At times when a person is faced with a predicament, he will vow to accomplish something for God if God will answer his plea for deliverance.

This has been classified a "fox-hole" religion, on the grounds that probably soldiers make vows to God while they are in combat that they find hard to satisfy when the war is over.

The present lesson covers an unfortunate period in Israel's history when God's people forgot their commitments to him. As we study the events, we have to remember the apostle Paul's command, "Therefore let any one who thinks that he stands take heed lest he fall" (I Cor. 10:12).

Whenever we make a promise to the Lord, our responsibility, our commitment will be tested. This lesson demonstrates how hard it was for the Israelites to be faithful to God.

The Consequences Of Disobedience
(Judg. 2:12-15)

Since there are three lessons taken from the book of Judges, it is important to think about the verifiable setting and reason for the book itself. Judges covers the period in Israel's history between Joshua's death and the rise of Samuel, about 1220 to 1050 B. C. It was a period of progress, when the dissipated (scattered) tribes were held together only by their common faith.

At the point when the people were faithful to God, they were effective as a nation, but turning to other gods brought shortcoming (weakness), division, and suffering. The book of Judges depicts various such periods. Be that as it may, when Israel's fortunes were at a low ebb, God sent deliverers, or judges, to lead the nation over its oppressors.

The stories of the exploits of these national legends (heroes) give the essential structure to the book. Six of twelve judges referenced are depicted in some detail. They were not made a judge in the modern sense of the word, but were men of action who wound up local or national rulers:

Spiritually, the Israelites entered Canaan as witnesses of God's great love and power and as recipients of his laws. They were to love only him and be a holy people, separate from the ways and traditions of different nations. The union of the twelve tribes shared a common faith and gathered around a common sanctuary.

In any case, plainly not all Israelites shared the lofty faith and vision of Moses, Joshua, and Caleb. The grumbling and disobedience that denoted the wilderness encounters were dismal omens of troble to come in Canaan.

Likewise, Israel's inability to eradicate the occupants of the land prompted genuine troubles later on. The Israelites were substance to settle down among the Canaanites and they lost the incentive to possess the whole land. Subsequently, God's people slowly ingested or absorbed Canaanite traditions, spouses, and false religion.

The record demonstrates that in spite of the fact that the judges were raised up by God to deliver Israel, none of them had the characteristics of Moses, Joshua, and Samuel. The triumphs of the judges are energizing, but flaws of character additionally stick out: Ehud was a fainthearted professional killer; Gideon drove the peoples

Dr. John Thomas Wylie

off track after his triumph; Jephthah was an entrepreneur; and Samson's endeavors dishearten as opposed to move us. Above all, there was little to check the drift away from the standards set in the law of Moses.

Israel Forsook The Lord
(v. 13)

The first chapter of Judges tells about the conquest of southern Canaan, including Jerusalem and Bethel. The author records (lists) the majority of the vacant region. The second chapter starts with the blessed messenger (angel) of the Lord confronting the people with proof of their unfaithfulness (infidelity).

At that point, before portraying Israel's present challenges, the author by method for complexity remembers Joshua's greatness (vv. 6-10). This paragraph causes us to comprehend both the idea of the conquest of Canaan and the heart of Israel's resulting failure during the times of the judges.

The campaigns under Joshua's leadership had crushed (broken) the spirit of Canaanite opposition (resistance), however a significant part of the local campaigning was left to the individual tribes. In this way, after the covenant renewing ceremony at Shechem, the tribes set about completing the occupation of their own allotted territory.

Joshua 23 clarifies that the tribes had a lot of hard battling to do before the land could appropriately be said to be conquered.

Joshua's influence can be found in Israel's loyalty to God during his lifetime and that of the elders who were associated with him (v. 7). Be that as it may, each generation must go into its very own vital spiritual experiences; it can't proceed in the spiritual strength of its past heroes.

Paganism was never far from the surface during this early period of Israel's history. Whenever Joshua and his contemporaries died, the new generation shared neither their faith nor their resolutions of the great deliverance wrought for them by the Lord (v. 10).

The remainder of chapter 2 is a summary of what follows in the book of Judges. Verses 11-23 set out the rehashed pattern of occasions that started once the generation of the conquest vanished (died out). The history of very almost two centuries is condensed, demonstrating the four phases of a recurring cycle; disobedience, slavery, supplication, and deliverance.

Fundamentally, the country forsook the Lord, a crime that included unfaithfulness (disloyalty) to their forefathers and disregarding the mighty works of the Lord on their behalf, particularly the deliverance from Egypt. God had given the Israelites sufficient proof for them to remain faithful to him, rather, they turned to the gods of the Canaanites.

Why? Likely on the grounds that the worship of these gods appeared to be all the more legitimately identified with their immediate wants for material flourishing.

For instance, note the gods referenced in v. 13, Baal and Ashtaroth. Baal, the child of El on the Canaanite system of gods, was god of the tempest (storm) and the rains and in this way the controller of crops and harvests.

Ashtaroth, the consort of Baal, was the goddess of war and ripeness (fertility). The religion of fertility gods was joined by a wide range of obscene practices. Male and female prostitutes were highlighted in customs that sought to promote the activity of the gods in nature. Once in a while child sacrifice was likewise included.

Believers today regularly wonder how God's people could move toward becoming captured in such false religion. Some portion of the appropriate response is found mixed marriages (3:5, 6). Additionally, at whenever two groups of people come into contact, there is a practically unavoidable tendency for the religions to become mixed.

On account of a conquered nation, the gods of that nation assume a substandard place (inferior) in the religion of the conquerors. Regularly this is definitely not a purposeful strategy (a deliberate policy) it simply happens unknowingly.

In any case, for what reason would the Israelites give any consideration to the gods of the Canaanites? This generation knew the narratives of how the Lord had provided for Israel in the wilderness, and how the Lord had given them triumphs under Joshua. Obviously, Jehovah was better than Baal. In any case, once in the land, they fell victim to the possibility that local gods - mediocre compared to Jehovah - controlled the rain and the harvests.

There was no cognizant deserting of God, however mixed marriages, the need to offer regard to nearby gods of fertility, and the arousing (sensual appeal) intrigue of Canaanite worship, were factors that prompted this defection from God's will.

The example set here was normal for the country until after the destruction of Jerusalem in 587 B. C. The prophets always rebuked the people for spiritual infidelity (spiritual adultery - "going after Baal" - a charge that was resisted by the people who unaware of the fact that they were not true worshipers of the Lord.

(What are some bogus gods, or false religions, that test God's people today? What reasons would you be able to discover for their appeal? By what method can the churches help people stay away from the snares of cultists?)

Israel Was Plundered
(v. 14)

God's people were gone over to their adversaries, that is, the people they had neglected to kill. The people of Israel were pillaged; they lost their property, their harvests, their domesticated animals, their families. In actuality, they turned into the captives of atheist tribes. They were weak against their adversaries.

The author ascribes this to God's indignation against Israel. God was not angry in a noxious manner; he was furious as befitted his own holiness and justice. Here is clear confirmation that God can't disregard sin in light of the character of his own temperament. God must pass judgment on sin.

Israel was harried, subjugated, and enfeebled as a result of the manifestation of the spiritual circumstances and logical results guideline.

God, obviously, used human variables to work out this judgment. Israel's spiritual strength was sapped by the sensual Baal love. This was joined by a comparing decrease in the good and physical imperativeness of the people. Shortcoming in the life of a country can be followed to fundamental spiritual infidelity. At the point when a people spurn the Lord, they become frail in different regions too.

God Was Against Israel
(v. 15)

Israel attempted to fight back against her oppressors, but it was no use, because God baffled her efforts. Israel had strong warriors, but God was against them. Here is another outcome of the country's departure from the covenant with God.

It was military calamity. Israel's judgment was lost and her armies were disrupted and divided. Once more, God's judgment had serious outcomes in regular everyday concerns.

In any case, God had warned Israel this would occur. During the time under Moses, when the laws were given, Israel was warned that rebellion would bring personal and national hardship and torment (suffering).

(In what ways would you be able to see God's anger demonstrated today? For what reason is it for God to be angry? How might you help a person see the spiritual principals of cause and effect working today? What are some of the consequences of disobeying God?)

The Spiritual Declension Of Israel
(Judges 2:16-19)

These verses summarize the subsequent 200 years. It is a dismal story, but then reassuring on account of what God accomplished for Israel. The picture was not absolutely dark.

God Raised Up Deliverers
(vv. 16, 18)

Here is God's intervention, which from ensuing records we know was incited by the cries of his people (cf. 3:9). The leaders, or judges, were raised up by the Lord essentially out of benevolence (mercy) for his people. They didn't deserve his help; God was "moved to feel sorry for by their groaning" under various oppressors.

The record of God's great love through these judges looks like this: Othniel of Judah against Cushan-rishathaim; Ehud of Benjamin against Eglon of Moab; Shamgar against the Philistines; Deborah of Ephraim and Baarak of Naphtali against Jabin and Sisera; Gideon of Manasseh against the Midianites and Amalekites; Tola of Issachar; Jair of Gilead; Jephthah of Gilead against the Ammonites; Ibzan of Bethlehem; Elon of Zebulum; and Samson of Dan against the Philistines.

These people received special powers and gifts from the Lord, which were used to deliver Israel from her enemies and after that to rule the people.

Dr. John Thomas Wylie

The People Served Other gods
(vv. 17, 19)

Here is the opposite side. The influence of the judges never lasted extremely long. God's merciful deliverances were soon forgotten. The people returned to idol worship. The spiritual authority/leadership of the judges was repudiated. Verse 17 shows that neither the godly example of their forefathers nor the commandments of the Lord had any effect on them.

The prevailing spirit is by all accounts one of stubborn rebellion against God, adhering to selfish desires and the norms of the encompassing pagan culture. When the immediate emergency (crisis) was finished (was over), they forgot both their prior wretchedness, misery and the state of temporary repentance. It appears the impression that their cries to the Lord were shallow (superficial) as opposed to genuine repentance.

It is conceivable to use God as an escape when challenges are rough. This is a peril today. Indeed, even countries think that its practical to call long periods of prayer, for instance, but when the crisis has passed, it has returned to the same old thing. People and churches can fall into the same trap.

God expected that Israel would show gratitude for deliverance by obeying his will. That is the principle of Christian discipleship as well. The New Testament says we are to yield ourselves to God because of his mercies (cf. Rom. 12:1, 2 NIV).

We need to remember as we take a look at this synopsis of life under the judges that the years of harmony (peace) and rest far dwarfed the long stretches of oppression. For instance, forty years of rest pursued the first oppression of eight years (3:8, 11 NIV); eighty years of rest pursued eighteen years of oppression (3:14, 30 NIV); forty years of rest pursued by twenty years of oppression (4:3; 5:31 NIV); forty years of rest pursued seven years of oppression (6:1;8:28 NIV).

(How would you account for Israel's short memory of God's deliverances? For what reason do we now and again center more around our "groanings," in a manner of speaking, than on our triumphs? How might we grow better spiritual memories of God's power and blessings?

Dr. John Thomas Wylie

What is proof that repentance is authentic? What people has God raised up to help you spiritually? Why cannot one generation live on the spiritual victories of the past?)

The Judgment Of God
(Judges 2:20-23 KJV)

Here is the spiritual background for what was going on in Israel during the time of the judges. This is a look at conditions from God's standpoint.

The Reasons For His Judgment
(v. 20)

It was not hard to find the source of the problem. God's people had broken their covenant promise with him and they had disobeyed his' words. In making the covenant they had consented to do all that he had commanded (Exod. 19:8 KJV), but the promise was not kept. The circumstance brings to mind the thing an advanced statesman said about treaties: "They are made to be broken."

The Test For Israel
(vv. 21-23)

God used the surviving countries in Canaan to test Israel. God had revealed to Joshua that he would be with him to drive out Israel's enemies. In any case, now God says that he won't oust the tribes that are left. Rather, they would stay as a test of Israel's loyalty and faithfulness.

Israel failed the test; the people ended up being unfaithful to the Lord. This is called spiritual harlotry (v. 17). God's relation with his people resembled the marriage bond and vow which Israel had broken.

The voice of Israel's conscience was dulled by progressive acts of disobedience. Rather than resist temptation presented by the surviving tribes, Israel succumbed and refused to walk in the way of the Lord.

It has been said that no place in Scripture is man's fundamental predisposition to sin more graphically depicted than in the book of Judges. This book likewise uncovers the root thought of sin; doing anything you desire to, autonomously of God's will (cf. 17:6; 21:25 KJV).

However that isn't the whole story of Judges. We also observe the wonder of God's constant love and concern even in the face of man's sin.

In spite of Israel's past unfaithfulness, and regardless of what God knows will happen once more, when the people went to him he answered. That should be a support to any person who is battling to be committed and faithful to the Lord.

Chapter Eleven

Renewing The Covenant
(Joshua 24:19-28 KJV)

IT BENEFITS US OCCASIONALLY to face times of commitment. Each time we hear a sermon, each time we listen to the teaching of a Sunday school lesson, and each time we read the Scripture we should consider a fitting response.

As a result, the Word of God demands a decision; decisions must be made; strategies settled on.

Else, we face the threat James depicts: "For if any one is a hearer of the word and not a doer, he is like a man who watches his natural face in a mirror; for he observes himself and goes away and at once forgets what he was like" (1:23, 24 KJV).

We need to be brought up short once in a while in view of proneness to absent mindedness (forgetfulness) and spiritual sluggishness (laziness). It is anything but difficult to slide into a simple, comfortable Christianity. That is the reason Peter advises: "Make every effort to supplement your faith..." (II Pet. 1:5 RSV).

Sadly, the Christian faith some of the time is thought about as one-time only responsibility (a one time commitment); you settle on a decision, take the church membership class (some call it the orientation class); get your name on the church roll, and that is it.

In any case, the adversary (Satan) of our souls tries constantly to subvert that choice. He needs us to skirt the intense good and moral necessities of Christian duty. He is enchanted when Christians experience life simply like non-
Christians.

In this way, in light of our own internal slackness and in view of Satan's strategies, we need challenges that will force us to decide who to follow and what to do. We ought to be happy when the pastor looks at us straight without flinching and instructs us to settle on a decision. Each aspect of our lives - our time, our cash, our work, our family relationships - must go under Jesus Christ's control.

In this lesson we will perceive how Joshua of old forced the people of Israel to confront an either-or-decision. If you attempt to straddle the fence with God, you truly are against him. Christians today need to think about the implications of saying yes to Jesus Christ.

The Consequences Of Commitment
(Josh. 24:19-24)

Chapters 23 and 24 establish Joshua's goodbye to the people he had served so faithfully. The great chief of the triumphs of Canaan was going to depart. It was a fitting time for him to offer praise to God and to challenge the Israelites "to love the Lord your God" (23:11 NIV).

Joshua helped them to remember God's faithfulness: "Not one thing has fizzled of the considerable number of things which the LORD your God had taken them from bondage in Egypt and had given them a home in Canaan and harvests to live on (24:6-13 KJV).

However, Joshua knew how simple it would be for the Israelites to return to the old paganism and to adopt the idolatries of the Canaanites, so he tested them legitimately: "Choose this day whom you will serve" (24:15). The people acknowledged God's protection and his provision; they professed their desire to serve him (vv. 16-18 KJV).

(Sequentially, the events of this lesson happened before the events of the past lesson. The conquest of Canaan is dated around 1240-1220

B.C. It is followed by the period of the judges, 1220-1050 B.C.)

Joshua's Warning
(vv. 19, 20)

Often in the emotion of stirring addresses, people make untimely or premature responses. This was an emotion-laden scene. The old warrior-leader was about to die. Joshua didn't delegate a successor. For him, the country's future relied upon a certain something: obedience to God's laws and faithfulness to him.

Joshua's past record was inspiring; he had not failed God's commands and God made good his promises. At the close of his formal address he had cried, "As for me and my house, we will serve the LORD."

Now the people had made the same declaration. Joshua was obliged to expound on what it meant to serve God. The essential question was nature of God himself. Before one can vow to serve him, one must know his demands. Nobody should make a promise to God before analyzing the character of God. What is God like?

Here, to make the issue obvious, Joshua singles out God's holiness. He is holy to such an extent that in the perfection of his character he can't overlook sin.

God's holiness is the flawlessness of his character in love, truth, justice, and righteousness. The Bible says, "God is light and in him there is no darkness at all" (I John 1:5 NIV).

He is a "jealous" God as in he can't tolerate mixed loyalties. You can't serve God and other gods. God's nature requires total faithfulness, allegiance and obedience. He isn't one among many gods; he is the supreme deity. Consequently, it is no light thing to worship and serve him.

Because God is holy and jealous, he can't tolerate sin. Disobedience and unfaithfulness to him must be punished. That is the purpose of Joshua's warning that God will not forgive sin. Joshua didn't state that God never forgives. Man's relationship to God depends upon forgiveness; forgiveness is always promised to the repentant sinner.

Joshua was addressing an immediate, specific danger; the blatant denial of God, forsaking him for other gods (v. 20 KJV) If that occurred, Israel would be punished. The people needed this warning, lest they think they could disobey God without punishment. That has consistently been a common thought: "Sure, we can sin. What of it?"

Israel's blessing in the land depended upon her obedience to God. The people couldn't feel that because God has blessed them before (in the past), he would bless them later on, regardless of what they did. This is explained clearly in 23:15, 16: "But just as all good things which the LORD your God promised concerning you have been fulfilled for you, so the LORD will bring upon all of you the evil things....if you transgress the covenant of the LORD your God...and go to serve other gods."

Judgment would come if the people forsook God. This warning that God would not forgive this sin is identified with a similar warning by Jesus in Matthew 12:31, 32, where he says there will be no forgiveness for those who blatantly ascribe to the evil one (Baalzebub) the deeds done by the mighty power of God.

Joshua warned the people that to ascribe to the Baals of Canaan the power which belonged to God alone was a sin which, persisted in, could not be forgiven.

(For what reason is it beneficial to warn people that it is not easy to serve God? What "cannots" did Jesus provide for the prospective disciples? Cf. Matt. 6:24; Luke 14:27. What occurs in the church when the expense of being a Christian is not expounded? How might we help people gain an accurate understanding of the nature of God?)

The People's Promise
(vv. 21, 22 KJV)

The people persisted in their declaration of obedience to God. It is good and wise to empower people to consider the consequences (count the cost), to confront the consequences of their decisions. There must be honest, calm, sober reflection (cf. Luke 14:28-33 KJV).

Obviously, there was passionate eagerness here, however in any event Joshua gave the people a opportunity to look at their response in the light of God's character. His holiness and his judgment of sin didn't prevent them from their desire to profess allegiance to him. This is the thing that God expects of his people today: consider the consequences (count the cost) and after that tell transparently and freely where you stand.

There is little opportunity today for the public at large to witness Christian declarations of faith and obedience. In certain nations, however, where Christians are a small minority, they regularly rampage in motorcades, parades, carrying pennants broadcasting their responsibility to Jesus Christ.

In Joshua's time, he couldn't appeal to some other people or gods as witnesses, so he spoke to the people themselves; he named them as witnesses of the covenant. They consented to this technique and acknowledged the commitment.

So today, in actuality, our duty to Christ depends on our promise (our word), but then it is a sign of good and spiritual fortitude to stand firm for Jesus Christ in an open gathering. Walking to the front of the church toward the end of an evangelistic meeting doesn't make a person a Christian. But if that person needs to say, "I will serve the Lord and receive Christ as my Savior," he should be eager to make that assertion in an open manner.

Was this an ill-advised choice? Were the individuals excessively rushed in noting Joshua's test? Maybe some were essentially carried alongside the enthusiasm of the day, however clearly others were confirming the genuine conclusions of their souls. Joshua was faithful in making God's demands obvious and many people were moved to profess their faithfulness and obedience to the Lord.

We need not stress over making the particulars of Christian teaching excessively steep. In the event that God is grinding away in the hearts of people, they will readily step out for him. That is one bit of leeway of calling for open responses. It strengthens the resolve of God's people and encourages others to trust him, as well.

Joshua's Command And The People's Response (vv. 23, 24 KJV)

Now a particular demonstration was called for. When a person vows or promises to do God's will, there will be a relating alteration (a change) in conduct. You can't say you're God's ally and after that lead the same old life. God's holiness demands changes in the style of life. If the changes are not made, one's calling is an untruth, a lie and Christianity turns out to be sheer hypocrisy.

A covenant with God is like an agreement with any other person: when you leave all necessary signatures, you promise to do certain things.

Here, the issue was "foreign gods," or idolatry. Something must be done right away. "Put them away," Joshua said. That was the negative side of commitment. The positive side was this: "Incline your heart to the LORD." There were evidently various secret barbarians (idolators) in the camp, as there were in the times of Jacob. This idolatry may have been the fire worship of their ancestors (cf. vv. 2, 14 KJV) or that of the native Cannanites.

A genuine response of God will consistently includes both "putting away of" and "putting on." This is clear from such a New Testament passage as Colossians 3:5-17. Corrupt practices must be deserted, abandoned by an act of the will, the heart must rest completely in God himself. To "incline" one's heart to the Lord means to trust in him personally and obey his commands (cf. John 14:21, 23 KJV).

There is no proof here indicating what the real worshipers of another god (idolaters) did. On certain events in the Bible the people disposed of their idols publicly. Paul commended the Thessalonians since they "turned to God from idols, to serve a living and true God" (I Thess. 1:9 KJV).

In many places where preachers and missionaries have taken the gospel, when the people trusted in Christ they brought out their idols and burned them.

In any case, the people again promised to serve and obey the Lord. This implies the extent that they could undeerstand it, they would not serve the gods (idols) of the Canaanites.

This was a successful screen (monitor) on the Israelites for a long time.

"Israel served the LORD all the days of Joshua, and all the days of the elders who outlived Joshua" (v. 31 KJV).

As we note in the past lesson, failure did come, but the picture was not absolutely dark. What Joshua did was vital and beneficial. He could only make the issue clear and articulate a strong appeal for faithfulness; he couldn't promise it. The church needs leaders to talk bluntly about the demands of Christian discipleship, despite the fact that the blessings of revivals and evangelistic meetings don't keep going forever.

(What opportunities do you need to make public affirmations of your desire to obey God? Does your church have an membership covenant? How regularly is it perused? Should your church have a yearly declaration of agreement with the covenant? Why or why not? In practical terms, what does it mean to serve God? Since Idolatry as such is not a problem, what things tend to get in the way of your total obedience to God? What do you need to "put away"?)

The Covenant Established
(Josh. 24:25-28 KJV)

This was the peak of Joshua's farewell. It was a grave minute. The entire country stood in the spotlight before God and before the encompassing nations.

The Israelites were to be God's light-bearers, the bearers of truth and holiness in a degenerate, corrupt, depraved world. Thusly, Joshua chose to make both a written and a public record of this earth shattering event.

The Covenant Ratified And Recorded
(vv. 25, 26a KJV)

"Joshua made a covenant" means he formalized the understanding they had quite recently made among themselves and God. Their understanding was general: "We will serve and obey the Lord." As noted above, it required first that they cut out their worship of other gods.

In any case, there were different ramifications also. These "statutes and ordinances" Joshua wrote in a book, which was known as the law of God. There would be a lasting record of the responsibility and commitment made by the people and the requirements of the Lord in lieu of that commitment. This book was placed "by the side of the ark of the covenant of the LORD" (Deu. 31:26 KJV).

We can express thankfulness toward God that in his insight he wanted to have his word written first and after that saved as the centuries progressed. We are not subject to verbal traditions, not on "cleverly devised myths" (II Pet. 1:16 KJV).

Tyrants often have smothered or suppressed the Bible, and in certain nations today copies of the Bible are rare, but God's word still offers light to all. No Christian need be uninformed about what God requires. At the point when a person trusts in Jesus Christ for his salvation, he puts himself under obligation and commitment to be obedient to God's Word written.

The Great Stone And Its Significance
(vv. 26b-28 KJV)

Joshua set up a great "witness" stone to help the people to remember what they had done and to show the unbelievers around them that they had made a solemn covenant with their God. This stone would be a silent rebuke to any person who withdrew (departed) from the agreement.

It was set up "in the sanctuary of the Lord" at Shechem, the spot where Abraham and Jacob had sacrificed and worshiped. Maybe the altar of Abraham and Jacob was all the while standing. As of late archaeologists have revealed an extraordinary limestone pillar at the site of Shechem.

Joshua's last warning was against the peril of double-crossing (betraying) the Lord. This was a personal note. The genuine love of God is certainly not an emblematic ritualistic ceremony, but a personal relationship dependent on trust and obedience. There is a living God in heaven whom anybody can know and serve.

The Bible reveals to us the conditions of this relationship. In the days of ancient Israel, God engaged with explicit acts to prove his reality. He sent leaders to guide the people in their response to the God who had along these lines acted.

In later occasions, God revealed what he resembles in the person of Jesus Christ. Through Christ's death and resurrection sin can be forgiven and eternal life obtained.

However to gain the advantages of what God has done in Jesus Christ, a person must go to that spot of trust and commitment. He must make an covenant, as it were, in return of his faith in Jesus Christ, God vows to forgive and to give eternal salvation.

Joshua's warning is appropriate today: "Beware lest you deal falsely with your God."

That is a sad error, but many people attempt to play this game with God. They want to live their very own lives however they see fit, but some way or another proclaim faith in God. Be that as it may, the covenant of commitment to Christ demands open obedience.

The spirit of Joshua and of believers during that time was communicated by William, Prince of Orange, when his life and property were undermined by the attacking despot, Philip of Spain. William announced: "I am in the hands of God. My common merchandise and my life have since a long time ago been devoted to his service. He will discard them as appears to be ideal to his glory and my salvation."

(What noteworthy spiritual achievements would you be able to review in your life? For what reason would they say they are significant at this point? Offer an involvement in which a choice you needed to make was molded by an open presentation or responsibility you had made a long time ago. Under what conditions could a Christian's calling of faith be a "witness against him"?" How would you be able to help children to make a knowledgeable commitment to Jesus Christ that will determine the course of their life?

"Do not rebel against the Lord," Joshua asked the people of Israel when they had their first opportunity to enter Canaan, but they refused

(Num. 14:9 KJV). That was his closing appeal and injuction. It serves us well moreover. It is something we have to hear day by day when we are tempted to hold back or disobey.

Chapter Twelve

Gideon: God's Courageous Man
(Judg. 7:2-8, 20, 21 KJV)

"YOU CAN'T FIGHT HALL" it is a slogan that regularly has interfered with the endeavors of people who want to see change in the public life. A similar frame of mind has also incapacitated Christians who often feel there is nothing they can do to battle the evils of the world. "What can a few of us do against the entrenched power of the wicked?" we regularly ask ourselves.

Subsequently, in light of the Christian's limited influence and power on the human level, nothing or next to nothing is done about many of the world's prevailing social ills from a Christian standpoint. There are many governmental programs at work today, yet the sheer immensity of the problems often strifles Christian initiative. This is definitely not a new situation. Someone has asked: "What can one man do?"

King David's companion Jonathan, who saidd, "Nothing can prevent the LORD from saving by many or by few" (I Sam. 14:6 KJV). In this lesson we study another man who lived by a similar standard, Gideon. He remains as an encouragement to the people who feel they need power to change things. Gideon demonstrates that a bold minority is more effective than an uncommitted majority.

The Call Of Gideon
(Judg. 6)

Gideon's story possesses the chapters in the book of Judges. Except for Samson, more space is given to Gideon than to any of the judges - twelve of them altogether.

The book of Judges gives meager data around eight of these leaders; only Deborah, Gideon, Jephthah, and Samson are given broadened treatment. Gideon was the fifth such deliverer to arrive on the scene. The time of the judges began around 1220 B. C. what's more, Gideon's vocation began around 1100 B. C.

Israel's fortunes pursued this cycle during this time; sin, mistreatment, oppression, repentance, and deliverance. Gideon was called by God to convey his people following seven years of oppression under the Midianites.

The Midianites were related to the Israelites. They were descended from Abraham through his wife Keturah (cf. Gen. 25:2 NIV). Midian was found south of Edom at the northern furthest point of the Gulf of Aqaba. (Consult a Bible Atlas to pursue the subtleties here.)

They were a semi-migrant or semi-nomadic people and they had allies who helped them in their strikes on Israel (6:3 KJV), the Amalekites, who occupied the region toward the south of Judah, and "the people of the East," a nomadic group from the Syrian desert.

These trespassers (invaders) used another "unmistakable advantage," the camel, against Israel (v. 5). In this chapter there is the principal documentation of the enormous scale use of this animal in a military campaign. It gave the Midianites the gigantic favorable position of an expedient, long-run battling drive; unmistakably this overwhelming monster struck terror in the hearts of the Israelites.

The intrusion of Israel was an annual occasion during the seven years of Midianite mistreatment and oppression. The intruders (invaders) came "with their cattle and their tents" (v. 5 KJV). They are envisioned as insects (locusts), demonstrating the supreme pulverization as they moved starting with one zone then onto the next.

The impact of these assaults (raids) was considerable; all agriculture was affected; herds and crops were ravaged, plundered making for lean winters; it wasn't safe to live in open villages and towns. The Israelites were forced into a crude primitive presence in the out of reach (inaccessible) mountain regions (v. 2 KJV).

It was in conditions like these that the angel of the Lord appeared to Gideon, a "mighty man of valor" (v. 12 KJV). The people had cried to God for relief and the Lord initially sent a prophet to rebuke them for their sin. At that point the holy messenger (angel) of the Lord reported to Gideon that he would be the one to "deliver Israel from the hand of Midian" (v. 14 KJV).

Gideon imagined that God had cast off his people. He couldn't accept there would be divine intercession. At that point when it was revealed that he was to be Israel's deliverer, he could hardly imagine that either.

He answered to the Lord, "How might I deliver Israel? Behold, my tribe is the weakest in Manasseh, and I am the least in my family." Little did Gideon know now how God was going to win a triumph for Israel out of this human shortcoming (weakness).

God basically reaffirmed his promise to Gideon; he would be with him and the Midianites would be vanquished. Yet, God's Word was sufficient for Gideon. He requested an indication, a sign of confirmation that the delivery person (messenger) truly was the representative of the Lord (v. 17 KJV).

So Gideon was convinced by a dramatic appearance of fire, and he worshiped the Lord (vv. 19-24 KJV). At that point the Lord gave him an intense task (a tough assignment). He was to tear down his father's altar of Baal, cut down the idol or Asherah, and build an altar to God.

Gideon obeyed, but he did as such during the night since he feared his father and the townspeople. This occurrence uncovers reality of the prophet's charge (vv. 7-10 KJV). Excessive idolatry was rampant in Israel, even while the people were crying to God for deliverance.

Strikingly, Gideon's father went to his defense when the townsmen wanted to murder Gideon. Joash thought of some commendable religious philosophy: if Baal is a genuine god, he could deal with Gideon himself. It is fascinating to know how Joash rung a bell about Baal. Clearly his son's unequivocal activity was a rebuke to him.

At that point again the Midianites attacked Israel, but this time something else occurred. "The Spirit of the LORD took possession of Gideon" and he mobilized the Israelites to fight at the Valley of Jezreel. This, obviously, was the critical capability that Gideon required.

Before the crucial battle Gideon was prepared by God's will. God currently endued his servant with power from a on high. Before the pivotal fight Gideon was set up by God's Holy Spirit. He was as yet the least in a family that was the weakest in the group, but he had what he expected to deeliver Israel: the Holy Spirit.

Be that as it may, on the eve of battle Gideon's faith required fortification (reinforcement). God had considered him a "mighty man of valor," but now Gideon requested an exceptional sign (a special sign) from the Lord that Israel would win the battle. God granted the sign.

Gideon acknowledged he was evading calamity, however he felt free to request one special sign. Once more, God in his benevolence gave Gideon his request (vv.36-40 KJV). Simply, this man required great mental fortitude (courage) to move out against such a well-furnished adversary. He realized that Israel was no counterpart for the Midianites and their allies. However, by one way or another he detected that God would accomplish something great. This is the reason he needed reassurance.

God didn't rebuke Gideon for his request. Every so often, Gideon's involvement with the fleece is cited to as a way to get guidance from the Lord today. We can't settle on a decision, so we request a sign from the Lord.

He recognized what he should do, but he didn't have the mental fortitude (courage) enough to do it. In this manner, he was truly requesting that God support his courage on the eve of a frightening venture against the Midianites.

(Request that a Christian companion portray the sort of person Gideon was. Did he have any strange qualifications for leadership? What does this recommend about anybody's potential? Compare the needs in Israel and needs you know about today. How can one get the mental fortitude (courage) to do great things for God? In what makes a difference can father and mother apply courage leadership? The children? What powers are free in the world today that tend to oppress

Christians? Where do we search for deliverance? from the Lord? Comment.)

Gideon's Fighting Minority
(Judg. 7:2-8 KJV)

In excess of thirty thousand battling men reacted to Gideon's call. Given the sadness of Israel's circumstance, this was an encouraging sign. Unquestionably Gideon probably been heartened. Be that as it may, he had no clue how God would pare his military down to only 300 men.

The Fearful And The
Trembling Return Home
(vv. 2, 3 KJV)

Gideon and his army took up positions at the spring of Harod at the foot of Mount Gilboa. Simply northwest, under five miles away, was the Midianite encampment by the slope of Moreth.

The Midianites clearly knew about Gideon and his army (cf. 7:14 KJV), however they were certain that they would win once more. They dwarfed the Israelites and brought a horde of camels along (v. 12 KJV). To any eyewitness of the scene, Israel would require each man she could marshal. In any case, God had other plans.

Gideon's army was to be diminished. In the first place, as per the arrangement of Deuteronomy 20:8, all of those who had no genuine heart for the fight were to be discharged. This was a legitimate standard, since fear is contagious and it can have a sad impact in battle. This is what befallen the Midianites (v. 21 KJV).

Be that as it may, how breaking and discouraging it probably had been for Gideon when more than 66% of his army - 22,000 out of 32,000 - melted away and returned home. Yet, God prepared his servant for this probability (v. 2 KJV).

God needed a small army, in case the Israelites brag of their own achievements. This is extremely the central point of the victory.

God's words focuses on that unimportant numbers themselves are no assurance of accomplishment (victory); it is the presence of the Lord that ensures victory, and he can work through a handful of dedicated people. The same truth is taught in the New Testament. The church was not begun by ground-breaking, powerful individuals.

The church itself grew out of a handful of people endowed

with the Holy Spirit. The apostle Paul explains: "Not many of you were wise according to worldly standards, not many were powerful, not many were of noble birth; but God chose what is foolish in the world to shame the wise; God chose what is weak in the world to shame the strong, God chose what is low and despised in the world, even things that are not, to bring to nothing things that are, so that no human being might boast in the presence of God"(I Cor. 1:26-29 RSV).

God wants the glory in victory, regardless of whether it be Israel's triumph over the Midianites, or our triumph over sin and death through faith in Jesus Christ. Paul needed to learn, as Gideon did, how this principle works. God had told Paul, "My grace is sufficient for you, for my power is made in perfect in weakness."

So Paul could say, "I will all the more gladly boast of my weakness, that the power of Christ may rest upon me. When I am weak, then I am strong" (II Cor. 12:9, 10 NIV). Gideon was about

to learn this principle by another strange test for
is remaining ten thousand men.

The Careless Are Sent Home
(vv. 4-8)

The first test was fundamental due to the significance of positive resolve in army, particularly one confronting such overpowering chances. The second test had to do with readiness (alertness) and the ability to be cautious about not being found caught off-guard.

Clearly, the majority of the men who answered Gideon's call knew nothing about soldiering. At the point when the rest was regulated, 9,700 fizzled and Gideon was left with just 300 hundred men. Those who were rejected were those who, tossing alert to the winds, dropped to their knees to drink. Those who were held were the individuals who essentially scooped some water out of the brook with their hands. As they drank they could be on the look out for enemy attacks; they would not be completely diverted by their drinking.

Envision how Gideon's heart sank when his army was diminished to 300, but the Lord had instructed him to send the others home, and he had promised a victory over the Midianites with just 300 men. However it more likely than not had been exceptionally hard for the leader to be left with such a small contingent of men to engage with the a huge number of Midianites in battle.

Now, be that as it may, Gideon was at that point planning an interesting procedure. Before he sent the people home, he commandeered their jars and trumpets. He required 300 of each. Clearly, he couldn't assault head-on, so he contrived a clever plan to capitalize on surprise.

The Holy Spirit's work is much in proof here. He took the frightful leader who requested two signs and gave him boldness and perseverence, even in the face of the loss of 31,700 men. At that point he (the Holy Spirit) gave him unusual wisdom (intelligence) for the battle.

However again God bolstered this man. "If you're still afraid," God said, "go to the Midianite camp and hear what they say." What he heard was exciting. One of the officers translated a dream as showing Israel's victory (vv. 13, 14).

Gideon's first reaction was famously all together (in order): he worshiped the Lord. He gave God the glory, he demonstrated his true

Dr. John Thomas Wylie

confidence and faith, and afterward he came back to encourage his men. This man was a genuine spiritual leader, as well as a clever general.

However, we can't ignore God's loving patience toward him at every turn. God was faithful to the promise he made when he first appeared to Gideon: "The Lord is with you."

Gideon's Victory
(Judg. 7:20, 21 NIV)

Most likely no army in history has ever progressed on an enemy with such a combination of gear: trumpets (made of cattle horns), torches, and pitchers. Gideon and his men progressed "toward the beginning of the middle watch" (i.e., around 10 P.M.). They were separated into three groups of one hundred men each, so they could encompass the camp of Midianites.

Gideon's plan was to have his men stand in place. To begin with, they impacted their trumpets, at that point they broke their pitchers, and afterward they yelled a powerful cry.

They kept on making however much clamor as could reasonably be expected, to add to the disarray. While they rotated trumpet impacts and rallying calls, the Midianites charged in absolute perplexity.

Likely the camels also loosened up and hustled through the camp. The warriors lashed out at one another, not realizing who was companion or adversary. The people who endure fled the grievous scene. Such was the result of sheer frenzy in the camp, achieved by the component of surprise and uncertainty.

Later on, while in quest for the adversary, Gideon experienced both hatred and an absence of hospitality from his kindred Israelites. The Ephraimites he appeased, yet the elders of Succoth he punished. In the flush of victory the Israelites offered Gideon the majesty (kingship), however he refused, calling attention to that Israel had no king but the Lord himself (8:23 KJV).

Nonetheless, Gideon succumbed to the temptation of idolatry. He failed the trial of success, using gold to make an ephod that turned into the object of idolatrous worship (8:24-28 KJV). When he died, the Israelites turned again to worship Baal (8:33 KJV) and they neglected to honor the memory of Gideon (8:35 KJV).

(Where were Gideon's qualities? His shortcomings? What individual consolation do you get from his life? What alerts/warnings? What gifts has the Holy Spirit given you? It is safe to say that you are searching for some difficult task from the Lord? How might you help encourage a committed minority to endeavor a critical task for the Lord?)

Last lesson: What is said of Gideon and other Bible heroes of faith that, in addition to other things, they "won strength out of weakness" and "put foreign armies to flight" (Heb. 11:34 RSV). Their faith is held up as an encouragement to us today. Obviously, they remained imperfect, their shortcomings, which is the reason God was glorified by their faith. For Gideon's situation, his faith must be seen in obedience to God's commands, first in his own backyard, and then on the military front.

This is often God's example with us. He doesn't give us the generalship of the military to begin with, but expects that we should be obedient, trusting armed force privates in any case. Gideon took a chance with his life at home, at that point proceeded to lead the country. God is searching for faithfulness in the insignificant details of life. Maybe if more Christians focused on these, we would see more daring endeavors of faith in bigger issues also.

Chapter Thirteen

Samson: Struggle Against Opposition
(Judg. 13:1; 16:23-30 KJV)

TO CERTAIN PEOPLE, SAMSON was a bounder who squandered his life on women; to other people, he was a man who squandered his strength on absurd stunts; to-all, he stands as a witness to the catastrophe that that comes to pass for the people who waste great potential for substandard or inferior purposes. Samson goes down as exhibit A of "what may have been.

In any case, squandered potential (wasted potential) isn't restricted to those who have great talent or strength. Every person born has a God-given potential to achieve something good and worthwhile with his or her life. Again and again we pardon ourselves for not achieving what God can do with a person's life.

Obviously, there are human components in progress. At the point when the creator William Faulkner was asked what it took to be a decent author, he answered: '99 percent talent, 99 percent discipline, and 99 percent work."

Samson had the talent, however he did not have the discipline. It is simpler to rationalize than it is to teach yourself and buckle down. Samson just squandered (wasted) his talent because he would not bring it under control.

Today, we have the advantages of education and opportunities that past ages have never had, but we find many individuals ready to drift through life, searching for the path of least resistance (the easy way out). A similar disposition (attitude) likewise sneaks into the church where we see people as too disorderly or too undisciplined to even think about using the open doors (opportunities) for spiritual growth and service.

There is freedom to worship and to witness, yet many people restrain (limit) themselves to one sermon in seven days. Jesus warned of a coming time when it would be past the point where it is possible to work. He urged discipline and sacrifice while the time was ripe. Christians, as well, can pass up many chances to serve the Lord, and their lives can go down as accounts of "what may have been."

Bondage To The Philistines
(Judg. 13 KJV)

Samson was the last of the twelve judges of Israel, 1070 B.C. He made a judged Israel for a

Dr. John Thomas Wylie

long time (twenty years) after the Philistines had oppressed them for forty years. His profession is given more space (four chapters) in the book of Judges than is given to any of the other deliverers.

Thus, he is the best known of them and his adventures have propelled even mainstream dramatizations and movies. Too often, be that as it may, the underlying spiritual factors are often completely overlooked.

God Judged Israel's Sin
(v. 1)

The people of Israel "did what was evil," which means fundamentally excessive admiration, the love of Baal and Ashtaroth. The country was enduring profoundly in light of the invasion of pagan gods.

The people couldn't mount adequate spiritual solidarity to lose excessive admiration of idol worship and comply with the commands of the Lord. It was a consistent battle to battle the impacts of the encompassing tribes.

God's plan for spiritual victory was given in his commands to Joshua: "Be strong and very courageous, being careful so do according to all the law which Moses my commanded you... You will meditate over it (the book of the law) day and night...and then you shall make your way prosperous (Josh. 1:7, 8 NIV).

This the people neglected to do, and subsequently they fell into idolatry. There was no secret regarding why they failed; it involved not using the weapons of spiritual fighting God had given them.

Since God is holy and righteous, he judges sin. The judgment upon Israel for this situation was bondage to the Philistines. These intruders were recently referenced to in Judges 3:31 and 10:7.

When the Israelites left Egypt the Philistines were widely settled along the waterfront segment of Palestine among Egypt and Gaza. The Israelites bypassed to maintain a strategic distance from them (Exod. 13:17 NIV) and didn't experience them during the victory.

In any case, when Joshua was an elderly person they were set up in five urban cities, Gaza, Ashkelon, Ashdod, Ekron, and Gath. From this time for some generations these people were used by God to chastise the Israelites.

Shamgar shocked them incidentally (3:31 KJV), but they always squeezed inland from the seaside plain. The Israelites adopted the gods of the Philistines (10:6), and as we shall see, there was inter-marriage between them.

The Philistines subdued Israel until the second battle of Ebenezer (I Sam. 7:10ff. ASV). Indeed, even before the end of the rule of King Saul they had infiltrated as far inland as Bethshan (I Sam. 31:10 ASV).

God Promised A Deliverer
(vv. 2-5 KJV)

There is no word here about repentance or crying to God for deliverance, as we found in our earlier lesson (6:6, 7 KJV) In any case, since this was the typical example, we can be sensibly sure this happened once more. What's more, it is obvious from this occurrence that not the majority of the Israelites had bowed the knee to Baal; Manoah and his significant other - Samson's parents - were run of the mill of many faithful families.

God declared to the spouse of Manoah (she isn't named) that despite the fact that she had been infertile (barren) until this time, she would now bear a son who would deliver Israel from the Philistines. Also, he was to be a "Nazirite to God." His mother needed to watch a portion of the Nazirite safety measures for now, particularly those relating to nourishment and drink.

The Nazirite vow was one of various special promises that an Israelite may take. It could be seen by the two people. It was intended to accommodate the separating of a person for some extraordinary assistance for the Lord. From Numbers 6:1-21 we become familiar with the regulations.

The Nazirite will undoubtedly go without liquor (alcohol) or anything that may ferment and create liquor, for example, wine, strong beverage, grape juice, and grapes crisp (fresh) or dried. The hair and facial hair (beard) were to stay whole during the time of the vow. The Nazirite was forbidden to touch a dead body, even on account of close relatives. The Nazirite vow was not a lasting promise, however was limited.

Samson's Godly Parents
(vv. 6-25 KJV)

The declaration by the angel of the Lord didn't set well with Manoah, but he needed to be certain that he and his better half obeyed verifiably. So he supplicated, "Return again to us, and encourage us what we are to do with the child that will be conceived" (v. 8). Here is proof of a God-fearing couple. They understood their need of heavenly help to be the parents of Israel's deliverer.

The angel rehashed his commands, however Manoah needed further affirmation, so he approached the holy angel for his name. The angel said his name is "wonderful," meaning "secret." Manoah then prepared an offering, and the angel vanished amidst the fire. They knew then that they had been conversing with the angel of the Lord.

Manoah's godliness is revealed in his fear that they would die because they had seen God. His significant other perceived that God intended to bless them, not kill them.

(How might you portray conditions in Israel? What pressures would make it hard for a family to keep up faith in God? What might people need to do to maintain their faith? What included pressure would be upon an person who needed to be a Nazirite? How are people set apart for the Lord today? What are the distinctive characteristics (distinguishing marks) of a Christian?)

Samson's Exploits
(Judg. 14; 15 KJV)

The following two chapters contain energizing stories, less of godliness and faith, but as of tricks and retribution. God used unusual approaches to complete his will, even as he did with Gideon and his pitchers, lamps, and trumpets.

Samson's Wedding
(Ch. 14)

Samson was honored as an adolescent (13:24 KJV) and the Holy Spirit started to use him against the Philistines (14:4 KJV). Strangely, the primary event got through Samson's frustration at his wedding.

Clearly this was not to be the customary sort of marriage, where case the bride would have come to live with Samson, however an alternate sort of relationship wherein the bride of the hour stayed with her own family, being visited by her significant other every once in a while.

At any rate, Samson's bride of the hour to-be gave away the secret of his enigma (riddle), and he got revenge on the town of Ashkelon. Her father offered her to Samson's best man, which prompted further an issue. In excess of a family quarrel was in question here, God used it to expedite judgment the people who were oppressing his people.

Samson's Harassment Of The Philistines (Ch. 15)

The force of the trouble mounted, and Samson won two fights with extraordinary death toll for the Philistines. It is intriguing that the people of Judah obviously were content with the Philistine domination. They resented the aggravation brought about by Samson's fight with them.

This episode demonstrates that Israel was not a firm national substance, however a free accumulation of envious tribes. During the hour of the judges, the oppression influenced a few tribes more than others.

In these two chapters certain realities stand out about Samson: (1) He was endued with powerful solidarity to beat men and beasts. (2) The Holy Spirit worked him up to alienate the Philistines. (3) Apparently he was faithful to his Nazirite promise during this time. (4) He

recognized his dependence upon the Lord, and
God inexplicably gave him water to drink. (5) He
built up a reputation for being a hero of renown
and as a leader of God's people.

Samson's Downfall
(Judg. 16 NIV)

Samson was riding the zenith of
accomplishment, but all of a sudden he capitulated
to a temptation that has caused the ruin of many
leaders history: an illicit affair with a woman.
This part makes pitiful reading, despite the fact
that in the end Samson's plea for another victory
was answered by the Lord.

Samson Gave The Secret Of
His Strength To Delilah
(vv. 1-17 KJV)

Samson's initially recorded immorality is
referenced in vv. 1-3 to make way for what happened
later with Delilah. The men of Gaza, the most
southerly city of the Philistines, knew Samson was
with a prostitute there, but Samson deceived them
and pulled down the doors of the city.

Samson at that point began to look all starry eyed at a Philistine woman in the valley of Sorek in the central mountains of Palestine. By and by the Philistines plotted to use his sexual weakness as a means for catching and murdering him.

They influenced Delilah to find Samson's source of strength as a end-result of eleven hundred bits of silver. That was almost thirty pounds of silver, or maybe about $2,500 at the present rates. The way that the leaders of the Philistines depended on guile, and the way that they offered such a gigantic fix, are smooth declaration to the regard and fear with which they saw Samson. He was in fact a threat to their control over Israel.

Delilah approached her selling out with chilly, cutthroat productivity. We wonder why Samson didn't catch on, but he isn't the first man who has allowed the gratification of passion to beat worries for security. Evidently his undertaking had been continuing for quite a while, with the goal that the Philistines could see the potential for catching him in it.

In the initial three endeavors made by Delilah, Samson embraced a fun loving, prodding disposition. The third endeavor was hazardously close to reality, for it concerned Samson's hair. This may uncover a stage descending, a debilitating in his purpose.

In the interim, Delilah persisted with her lip service, claiming to love Samson while plotting his demise. She completed her strategic bit by bit expanding the tone of her grievance when Samson mocked her.

At last, Samson collapsed before Delilah's interests. She never let up and "his soul was vexed to death." An impressive time frame go between every episode. Samson made repeated visits to have intercourse with Delilah, but she was not prevented from her brutal plan. Finally he revealed the source of his strength and revealed his Nazirite promise.

His hair itself was not the source of his strength. It was only a symbol of his separation to the Lord. His strength originated from God because of a surprising appearance of the Holy Spirit upon him. However Samson realized that on the off chance that he betrayed his vow, God would remove his strength. Indeed, even while he was entertaining himself explicitly, he could recall his dependence upon God for strength.

Samson Toiled In Slavery
(vv. 18-22 KJV)

Samson's strength was diminished to ineptitude. Quieted to sleep by Delilah, he was shaved by the Philistines. Indeed, as in the past, Delilah yelled, "The Philistines are upon you," but this time Samson's strength was no more. "The LORD had left him."

This is probably the saddest proclamation in the Bible. Samson didn't have the foggiest idea what had occurred. His hair was gone, his strength was gone; his God was no gone. In this manner, he was seized by his enemies and they tormented him and made a slave out of him.

The great warrior of Israel was blinded, bound, and made to pull grindstones (millstones). This essentially added to his humiliation.

In any case, while his captors made Samson secure with chains (fetters) of bronze around his hands and feet, oddly enough they didn't take care to see that he was shaved routinely. They maybe thought they don't have anything to fear from this visually impaired (blind) detainee. But, Samson's hair grew and so did his strength.

Samson Was Ridiculed At
A Pagan Festival
(vv. 23-27 KJV)

At some point after Samson's capture the Philistines held a service of thanksgiving to Dagon, to whom they credited triumph over Samson. Dagon was the main god of the Philistines, a god of vegetation. Samson's notoriety for dread and pulverization was noted at this festival. He was the "ravager" of the Philistines who had slaughtered a significant number of them.

Ordinarily at such celebrations after the wine streamed for some time the group would deteriorate into depravity, but this time somebody thought of Samson. The group took an increasingly vicious turn and Samson was acquired to "make sport for us."

They needed him to put on a show so they could scorn him further. Perhaps they needed Samson to entertain them with the sort of show we would connect with a strong man at a circus or carnival. The Philistines, who once dreaded the great hero, gave him to a youth, but the fellow was to be what Samson needed. He showed Samson where the pillars of the building were. This was an

Dr. John Thomas Wylie

pagan temple and the authorities and dignitaries sat in a secured (covered) portion overlooking a countryyard where Samson was performing.

The wooden columns (pillars) upheld the rooftop on which the horde of 3,000 was assembled. Samson knew the place and figured out a plan. He was brought "between the pillars" so his tormentors could get a more closer look at him.

Samson Destroyed The Philistines In His Death (vv. 28-30 KJV)

At the advantageous minute Samson shouted out to God. During his bondage he without a doubt repented of what he had done. He knew that God alone could answer him. He appealed to God for strength just one more time, so he could pick up vengeance.

God allowed Samson's request. He had to get a handle on two center columns. As the crowd above squeezed forward, Samson leaned in upon the columns and moved them off their stone bases. Samson asked to die in the breakdown (collapse) of the building.

When the rooftop gave way, many were killed right away, while others died in the resulting alarm. The definite number of setbacks isn't given, but they were more than Samson had killed in his lifetime, which at a traditionalist gauge would be eleven hundred (14:19; 8, 15 KJV).

Samson was buried in the hill country overlooking the valley of Sorek, the area of some of his most prominent endeavors and most servile disappointments.

(How might you assess Samson's life? His strengths? His weaknesses? What do you think he achieved for Israel? What exactly would you attribute to his defeat? What are a portion of the products of wayward living today? What could a Christian gain from Samson? When do you think you are particularly defenseless? What would it be a good idea for you to do about it? How does God strengthen his people today?)

Samson's life, which promised so much, was cursed and at last demolished by his arousing interests and absence of genuine partition to the Lord. God used him in a measure to complete judgment on Israel's enemies, but those triumphs just leave us asking what more he may have achieved for the Lord had he not fallen into sin.

Comparative problems face God's people today. We are encompassed by temptations of numerous types. God's people likewise are helped by leaders who stand firm from under different attacks.

The Holy Spirit is accessible today for spiritual endeavors, which need not be breathtaking, but which must spring from discipline and faith.

Chapter Fourteen

Prologue To Nationhood:
Give Us A King
(I Sam. 8:1-9; 10:1 KJV)

THE STRAIN OR PRESSURE to fit in (or conform) with the overall principles of society is exceptionally strong. Nobody likes to stand out in contrast to everyone else. It is hard to buck the tide and be a person. At times, if an person misbehaves, he can wind up mistreated by the people. Or on the other hand, if your conclusion is excessively troublesome, you may wind up compelled to be peaceful.

As a specialist once noted, "In its distraction with congruity, the world might be blameworthy of locking up its masters and honoring its mediocritics."

For the most part, notwithstanding, in our very own neighborhoods we might want to fit in (or conform) with the remainder of the people, as opposed to being particular. This propensity makes the Christian settle on some troublesome decisions about his style of life.

The Bible says of Christians, "Yet you are a chosen race, a royal priesthood, a holy nation, God's own people, that you may declare the wonderful deeds of him who called you out of darkness into his marvelous light" (I Pet. 2:9 NIV).

Jesus taught his disciples that they risked being persecuted in light of their identifying with him. Christians have paid an overwhelming cost for being unique. Today is the same; the Christian is caught between the strain to resemble other people and his desire to stand out distinctively for Jesus Christ.

God's ancient people Israel should be diverse (different) too. There was to be a sharp cleavage between their conduct and that of the surrounding people.

Israel was to worship the one true God and to obey his moral commands. In any case, this was difficult, in light of the fact that it made the Israelites stand out as peculiar people.

In the present lesson we will find that it was out of a longing, a desire to fit in or conform to the ways of surrounding nations that the Israelites demanded their very own king. God's people today need to check the motives behind their requests, lest we wind up being inspired and formed by the patterns or trends of the times.

The Request For A King
(I Sam. 8:1-6 KJV)

The setting of this lesson pursues by only a few years the scene of Samson and the Philistines. In the closing section of Judges, the essayist turns from Israel's saints to depict two episodes that show the low condition of religion and morality in Israel when "each man did what was right in his own eyes" (17:6 KJV).

This dark scene was lit up by the appearance of Samuel, who was both a prophet and a judge (I Sam. 3:20; 7:15 NIV). He was the connection between the times of anarchy and the monarchy. Like Samson, Samuel additionally originated from a faithful family and he likewise was committed to the Lord as a Nazirite (1:11 RSV).

While serving Eli the priest, Samuel heard God's call. His first prophetic message was one of judgment for Eli due to the sins of his sons. The nation of Israel, in the mean time, kept on engaging the Philistines, who captured the ark of God.

The ark was Israel's most valuable belonging, the point of convergence of the tabernacle worship. A duplicate of the law was kept inside it. Its cover was the leniency situate, the symbol of God's presence.

In any case, God sent a plague on the Philistines and they returned the ark. After twenty years (7:2 KJV) a genuine revival broke out in Israel. The old symbols - Baal and Ashtaroth - were obliterated. Samuel led the nation in repentance and cleansing.

Therefore, in the following battle with the Philistines, the Israelites emerged victorious (7:10, 11 KJV). Israel regained the upper hand during the times of Samuel, and later on Saul and David both kept the Philistines under control, until the great battle of Gilboa when Saul and Jonathan lost their lives.

Samuel's ministry included the vast majority of Saul's rule. He likewise annointed David to be Israel's second king (16:13 KJV). These were tumultuous days and Samuel had many opportunities to provide basic spiritual guidance to the nation.

Samuel's Unjust Sons
(vv. 1-3)

Samuel's two sons were delegated made judges in Beer-sheba, but not at all like their father they didn't exercise justice. They "didn't walk in his ways," but were inspired by personal gain, so they accepted hush money (bribes). Shockingly, they turned out a little better than Eli's sons.

Samuel was now around fifty-four years of age and evidently in view of his age he couldn't keep on making the circuit of Israel (7:16). In this way he restricted himself to what he could do at home (Ramah), and along these lines his sons were locked in to administer justice in outlying areas. Beer-sheba was at the southern extremity of Palestine.

The frequent unsuitability of human succession is a repetitive subject of Old Testament history, from Gideon's sons to the descendants of David. No big surprise then that Moses put such great stress on teaching godliness to our children (Deu. 6:4-9 KJV).

We don't know precisely why Samuel's sons succumbed to corruption. Nonetheless, their position implied they confronted more than the typical temptations of life.

The People Wanted A King
(vv. 4, 5)

The sins of Samuel's sons gave a guise to the elders of Israel to come to Samuel and demand a king. The leading men of the nation went to his home with a formal demand for an adjustment in government. The elders pointed to the age of Samuel, the untrustworthiness of his children, and the government of other nations as explanations behind their request.

Samuel's age and the failure of his sons brought to a head a movement that had been working up for quite a while. From a political outlook, the interest of the elders was a sensible one.

Israel had suffered under the restricted and occasional authority of the judges. There was disunity and desire between the tribes. Israel needed strength and the tribal leaders accused this for the absence of authority or lack of leadership.

Also, there was the consistent danger of the Philistines and the pressure to be like other nations. These people had kings, so why not

Dr. John Thomas Wylie

Israel? For what reason should Israel be unique, or different? Afterward, the people rehashed these reasons (8:20).

They blamed their issues for not having a king to oversee and to lead them in battle. As we will see, there was a deeper spiritual reason for this movement for a king to succeed Samuel and his sons.

Samuel Was Upset
(v. 6)

Obviously, this interest was no compliment to Samuel. His sentiments were harmed at the slight put upon him. "Displeased" signifies a more grounded inclination: outraged, irateness, anger, indignation, and revulsion. He was influenced by personal and family emotions, and furthermore by the progressive revolutionary idea of the change.

He realized how simple it would be for the people to spurn, forsake the living God, he realized how simple it was for the Israelites just to ape the government as well as the religion of other nations. The longing desire to be like other nations was in itself a sign of apostasy.

Be that as it may, Samuel didn't fight back. Rather, he prayed. His judgment was in danger of being swayed by emotions. It is simple for one's thinking to be obscured by the sentiments of resentment.

This is a beautiful case of how prayer can be used to gain self-control and sound judgment coordinated by the Holy Spirit. We would have less trouble taking care of differences in the church if we prayed out our emotions first.

(What sort of an individual do you think Samuel was? What potential reasons might you be able to recommend for the defection of his sons? What does their case uncover about our responsibility to judges today? For what reason was having a king appealing to Israel's elders? What things have you wanted on the grounds that another person had them? Has personal hurt ever blurred your judgment? What would you be able to do when you are tempted to respond based on your feelings?

God's Interpretation Of The Request
(I Sam. 8:7-9 NKJV)

God was directly concerned by this new turn of events. Here was a significant departure in

Israel's history and government. The old prophet and judge was on the spot, however God heard and addressed Samuel's prayer. God's answer, in one way, gives off an impression of being surprising, but it was not without rebuke and warning.

The People Had Rejected God's Rulership (vv. 7, 8)

Samuel more likely than not had been shocked by the Lord's answer. Samuel realized that the appointment of a visible king would fundamentally prompt the country's forgetting its unseen King in heaven.

However God instructed him to do what the people wanted. And yet, the Lord confirmed the spiritual issue that was at the root of the movement for a king.

The elders had not rejected Samuel - despite the fact that that could have effectively been the importance of their activity - however they rejected God himself. Samuel's wounded sentiments were calmed by this comparison.

It was one thing to be ungrateful for his long periods of unwavering, devoted leadership; it was something of a far higher size for the people to reject God. The Lord's answer helped Samuel to place the issue in the correct point of view.

At that point, God clarified a further principle in v. 8. Samuel was being dealt with the manner in which the Israelites had treated the Lord himself as far back as he had delivered Israel from Egypt. The elders of Israel had not started a movement of rejection with the interest for a king; this was the peak of a consistent example of rejection.

"They have rejected me from the day I brought them up out of Egypt," God said. So Samuel would place his very own rejection in the light of that a much larger spiritual concern.

Israel had rejected the Lord to serve other gods; presently the elders were forsaking the Lord to have a king. The standard of a king would not really mean the rejection of God. God could be obeyed and loved under that type of government. This was not a political issue; there were spiritual concerns that the elders couldn't get a handle on.

The proof of the past was limited by the elders in their endeavors to discover a government and king that would take care of their issues. Israel's defeats had been brought about by their defiance to the Lord, not just by an inappropriate arrangement of government.

God had carried judges to lead the individuals, however the elders felt that kings would be better. The rule of kings implies the foundation of lines, there would be progression in government.

The elders could have demonstrated new devotion and dependence upon God as the path for peace and security later on. Rather than gaining from the past, they decided that stable leadership would end the cycle of high points and low points under the judges.

This choice on their part shown an endeavor to bypass the Lord. In spite of the fact that they were willing to allow God, through Samuel, to choose their first king, they were basically rejecting God's leadership in the future.

The Request Was Granted
With A Warning
(v. 9)

God allowed the people to have their way, but he advised Samuel to disclose to them what might occur under kings later on. Since the elders clearly were intrigued exclusively in political practicality, at that point the political ramifications of their solicitation are to be put before them reasonably and unequivocally.

What might it mean to have a king? They have only to take a look at neighboring nations to find out: induction, forced labor, taxes, and the loss of personal freedom (vv. 10-18). In any case, this warning didn't discourage the people. When they made up their minds to have a king, there was no turning back.

It frequently has been called attention to that under King Solomon the people of Israel really came to know what Samuel warned them about here. But, students of history have found that different countries before Solomon's time likewise had harsh experience of the expense of having a monarchy government.

The people responded with new determination to have a king, so Samuel carried the issue to the Lord again. God emphasized to Samuel what his answer was: "Make them a king." So the issue was settled and the people got what they wanted.

Israel's First King
(I Sam. 10:1 NKJV)

God not only enabled Israel to have a ruler, he likewise guided Samuel to the man. His name was Saul and he was tall and attractive (handsome

(9:2 NIV). God also revealed to Samuel why he was choosing Saul; "He will save my people from the hand of the Philistines; for I have seen the affliction of my people, because their cry has come to me" (9:16 NIV).

Again the leniency (mercy) of God is poured out on an undeserving people. Saul is to be above all else and to crush Israel's adversaries. God has no interest for the desire of the rebellious elders to ape other countries, but he will respond to the cry of the ordinary people for relief from the Philistines.

Most likely after the long end of trouble indicated by 7:13 the Philistines started to threaten once more. Their move may have been connected with Samuel's seniority (old age) and his powerlessness to lead Israel as in the past.

At any rate, there was a genuine component in Israel that perceived that God alone could deliver them, king or no king. They were faithful in prayer and in obedience to God. His eye and heart are ever open to the call of faith, so he responded, using the king to-be as his instrument of deliverance.

This prophetic disclosure of the Lord to Samuel was thusly passed on to Saul at his anointing. Saul, obviously, had no clue what was happening. He was shocked at Samuel's action, and the prophet's words, as an inquiry, are planned to answer Saul's bewilderment.

"Why an I being anointed?" would be the normal inquiry. Samuel clarifies that God has done the choosing, not himself nor the elders. What's more, God had given him a particular task to save his people from their adversaries. At that point, to answer Saul's likely questions about the authenticity of Samuel's deed and proclamation, Samuel enlightened him (told him) concerning the signs that would verify the entire game plan as miraculous and God-given. "And every one of these signs came to pass" (10:9 NKJV).

The anointing depicted here was absolutely a private issue, not by any means was Saul's servant allowed to witness it. The nation had yet to "choose" Saul by other means, and this event is depicted in 10:17-27. The private anointing implied that Saul was set apart by God for kingly office and it was also the means by which kingly powers were granted. From this time on - ever after his rejection - Saul was irrevocably the anointed of God.

At Saul's public inauguration Samuel again rebuked the people for rejecting the God "who saves you from every one of your calamities and your troubles" (10:19). This shows again that the essential need in Israel was not political but rather spiritual. The certainty of the individuals must be in God himself, in no earthly leader, regardless of whether he be a judge or king.

For the following 120 years Israel was a bound together (unified) monarchy under Saul, David, and Solomon. However, at that point civil war broke out and the kingdom was divided between the ten tribes in the north (Israel) and the two in the south (Judah).

Those in the north suffered grievously under a succession of mischievous, wicked, idolatrous kings. In the south, there were a few faithful kings. The north made due until 722 B.C. also, the south until 586 B.C.

Israel's spiritual record under the monarchy was no better than anyone might have expected. Under David and Solomon, the country made extraordinary walks in financial and military power, but after that there was unfaltering decay and the people were compromising continually either by civil war or foreign invaders.

God granted the people their desire, but over the long haul having their way solved nothing.

(For what reason is it simpler to search for human answers for our issues than to trust in God for the appropriate response? For what reason would we say we are inclined to search for answers as far as earthly factors instead of from a spiritual perspective? For what reason are human explanations behind our decisions not really the right reasons? In what manner can a Christian keep his thought processes in accordance with God's will? What would you be able to do to keep from falling into the snare of needing your own particular way so unequivocally that you disregard or reject God's will?)

Conclusion: Israel wanted a king for deliverance, security, leadership, and pride. For each situation, God would have given what they needed. He had delivered them from oppressors and he promised security in the event that they would obey him. He could lead them to prosperity and blessing. As far a

Dr. John Thomas Wylie

pride is concerned, God himself is the believer's pride. "Let him who glories glory in this, that he understands and knows me....says the LORD" (Jer. 9:24 NKJV).

Bibliography

The Holy Bible (1964) Authorized King James Version. Chicago, Ill.: J. G. Ferguson

The Holy Bible (1982) New International Version. Grand Rapids, MI.: Thomas Nelson (Used By Permission)

The Holy Bible (1978) New York, NY.: New York International Bible Society (Used By Permission)

The Holy Bible (1953) The Revised Standard Version. Nashville, TN.: Thomas Nelson & Sons (Used By Permission)

The Holy Bible (1901) The American Standard Version. Nashville, TN.: Thomas Nelson (Used By Permission)

The Holy Bible (1959) The Berkeley Version. Grand Rapids, MI.: Zondervan (Used By Permission)

The Holy Bible (1977) The New American Standard Bible. USA.: The Lockman Foundation (Used By Permission)

The New Testament In The Language Of The People (1937, 1949) Chicago, Ill.: Charles B. Williams, Bruce Humphries, Inc, The Moody Bible Institute (Used By Permission)

The Wycliff Bible Commentary (1962, 1968) Nashville, TN.: Chicago, Ill.: The Southwestern Company, The Moody Bible Institute Of Chicago

Gutake, M. G. (1974) Plain Talk On Exodus. Nashville, TN.: Zondervan

Hunter, J. (1975) Judges And A Permissive Society. Nashville, TN.: Zondervan

Motyer, J. A. (2005) The Message Of Exodus: The Days Of Our Pilgrimage (The Bible Speaks Today Old Testament Series) Downers, Ill.: IVP Acadenic, Intervarsity Press

Wood, L. (1975) Distressing Days Of The Judges Nashville, TN.: Zondervan

About The Author

THE REVEREND DR. JOHN Thomas Wylie is one who has dedicated his life to the work of God's Service, the service of others; and being a powerful witness for the Gospel of Our Lord and Savior Jesus Christ. Dr. Wylie was called into the Gospel Ministry June 1979, whereby in that same year he entered The American Baptist College of the American Baptist Theological Seminary, Nashville, Tennessee.

As a young Seminarian, he read every book available to him that would help him better his understanding of God as well as God's plan of Salvation and the Christian Faith. He made a commitment as a promising student that he would inspire others as God inspires him. He understood early in his ministry that we live in times where people question not only who God is; but whether miracles are real, whether or not man can make a change, and who the enemy is or if the enemy truly exists.

Dr. Wylie carried out his commitment to God, which has been one of excellence which led to his earning his Bachelors of Arts in Bible/Theology/Pastoral Studies. Faithful and obedient to the call of God, he continued to matriculate in his studies earning his Masters of Ministry from Emmanuel Bible College, Nashville, Tennessee & Emmanuel Bible College, Rossville, Georgia. Still, inspired to please the Lord and do that which is well

– pleasing in the Lord's sight, Dr. Wylie recently on March 2006, completed his Masters of Education degree with a concentration in Instructional Technology earned at The American Intercontinental University, Holloman Estates, Illinois. Dr. Wylie also previous to this, earned his Education Specialist Degree from Jones International University, Centennial, Colorado and his Doctorate of Theology from The Holy Trinity College and Seminary, St. Petersburg, Florida.

Dr. Wylie has served in the capacity of pastor at two congregations in Middle Tennessee and Southern Tennessee, as well as served as an Evangelistic Preacher, Teacher, Chaplain, Christian Educator, and finally a published author, writer of many great inspirational Christian Publications such as his first publication:

"Only One God: Who Is He?" – published August 2002 via formally 1ˢᵗ books library (which is now AuthorHouse Book Publishers located in Bloomington Indiana & Milton Keynes, United Kingdom) which caught the attention of **The Atlanta Journal Constitution Newspaper.**

Dr. Wylie is happily married to Angel G. Wylie, a retired Dekalb Elementary School teacher who loves to work with the very young children and who always encourages her husband to move forward in the Name of Jesus Christ. They have Four children, 11 grand children and one great-grandson all of whom they are very proud. Both Dr. Wylie and Angela Wylie serve as members of the Salem Baptist Church, located in

Lilburn, Georgia, where the Reverend Dr. Richard B. Haynes is Senior pastor.

Dr. Wylie has stated of his wife: "she knows the charm and beauty of sincerity, goodness, and purity through Jesus Christ. Yes, she is a Christian and realizes the true meaning of loveliness as the reflection is her life of holy living gives new meaning, hope, and purpose to that of her husband, her children, others may say of her, "Behold the handmaiden of the Lord." A Servant of Jesus Christ!

Printed in the United States
By Bookmasters